French Chic

CHILDREN'S CLOTHES

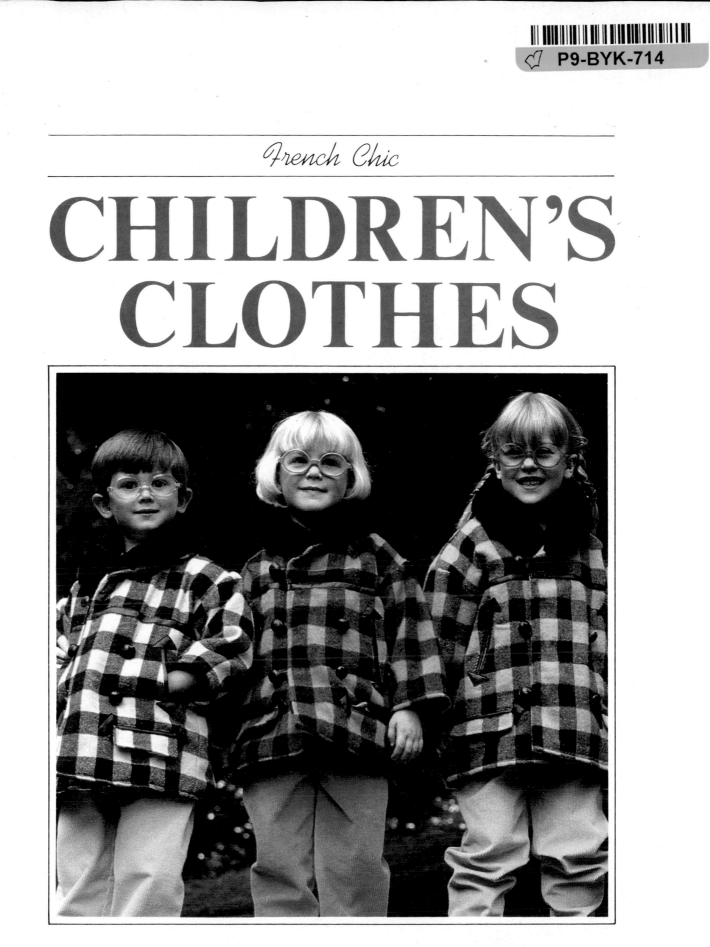

100 IDEES

BALLANTINE BOOKS · NEW YORK

Contributing Editor: Hilary More
Art Editor: Caroline Courtney
Text Editor: Mary Trewby
Design Assistant: Caroline Pickles
Illustrators: Caroline Pickles, Colin Salmon,
Cooper West

All of the designs in this book call for making your own patterns using pattern paper that professional dressmakers use.

Check your local sewing store to see if it carries pattern paper. If not, you may write or call the following for information on obtaining the pattern paper necessary to complete the designs in this book:

Enlarge-A-Design   (800) 526-7893 toll free
Stacey Industries   (201) 779-1121 in N.J.
38 Passaic Street
Box 395
Wood-Ridge, N.J. 07075

Conceived, designed and produced by
Conran Octopus Limited
28-32 Shelton Street
London WC2 9PH

Library of Congress Catalog Card Number: 85-91563

ISBN 0-345-33607-0

Manufactured in Hong Kong

First American Edition: August 1986

10 9 8 7 6 5 4 3 2 1

CONTENTS

INTRODUCTION

Children's clothes are fun to make, and quick too. With these patterns you will be able to make up modern designs, which are often hard to find in the shops. There are no hard and fast rules to observe when sewing for children, but if you follow a few guidelines you will be more than pleased with the end results.

Kids love to dig in the garden and meal times are always a hazard for the clothes of young eaters, so what they wear must be able to withstand wear and tear and lots of washing! Choose easy-wear, easy-care fabrics – cottons and synthetic mixtures are ideal, and they're easy to sew too. Always use a thread that matches the type of fabric and try to stick to simple fastenings – snap fasteners or self-ties – good for small fingers they are easy to apply to fabric. Remember that children grow quickly, so lengthen the life of pants by making them extra long and simply rolling them up – the continental look. Children love bright colors, so bear this in mind when shopping for fabric – try the drapery fabric department for large prints, which are a fun alternative to ginghams and stripes. And as children's clothes need little fabric, it's a great way to use up odd remnants.

Each pattern is accompanied by a set of easy-to-follow instructions, so you just can't go wrong when making these up-to-the-minute designs.

THE BASIC ESSENTIALS

ENLARGING A GRID PATTERN

The easiest way to enlarge a grid pattern is to use dressmakers' pattern paper, which comes ruled with ½in (1.2cm) squares; darker lines mark out the 2in (5cm) squares. One square on the pattern will equal a given measurement – for example, '1 square = 2in (5cm)'.

▦ Select a starting point on the pattern, then mark a corresponding point on the pattern paper. Find the adjacent point on the pattern and mark the same point on the paper. Continue carefully round the pattern, marking out the squares until the complete pattern emerges. Where the lines are straight simply join them with a ruler. Where the line is curved, plot round the lines and join them together freehand. Then simply cut out the pattern piece.

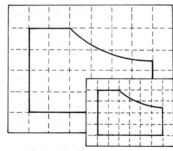

HOW TO ALTER A PAPER PATTERN

▦ All the paper patterns in this book can be altered to fit.
▦ First mark where the patterns can be altered. The bodice length should be altered below the chest line, and the width on a line from the center of the shoulder to the waist. To alter the skirt mark a line across between the hip and hem for the length, and a line centrally placed from waist to hem for adjusting the width. A sleeve length is altered in equal amounts from above and below the elbow. Mark a central line from top to wrist to change the width. The length of pants is altered between the crotch and hem, and for the width mark a central line from waist to hem.

▦ Once these adjusting lines have been marked, enlarge the pattern, by simply cutting along the marked lines. Move the two halves apart from the required amount and glue a strip of paper behind to join the two halves.
▦ When altering the width of a sleeve cap, the armhole size will have to be enlarged. Cut away a small amount from the top of the armhole edges of both front and back bodice, tapering the new lines to the original edges.
▦ To reduce a pattern, pin a tuck to remove the required amount along the marked adjusting lines on all the pattern pieces. In some cases the side edges of the pattern will have to be re-drawn to correct the distortion. If the sleeve cap is reduced in size, the armhole edges of both front and back bodice will have to be reduced again taper the edges to the original pattern edges.

CUTTING OUT THE PATTERNS

Before you begin it's important to straighten the cross grain of the fabric. Plain woven cottons or cotton blends should be torn, not cut, when you buy them, otherwise, to straighten the ends simply snip into the selvage and tear across the fabric from one side to the other. On heavier, woven fabrics such as wools or linens, snip into the selvage and pull out one thread clear across the fabric. Cut across the fabric along the marked gap. On knits use a large tailor's square placed against the selvage and a ruler and simply mark across the fabric.
▦ Fold the fabric in half lengthwise with all edges aligned. If there is distortion, pull the fabric diagonally from corner to corner. Press the fabric to remove any creases.
▦ When the pattern pieces need to be placed against a fabric fold, fold the fabric with the grain lines parallel to the selvages.
▦ If the fabric has a distinctive pattern or motif, try to center the main motifs on the main parts of the garments. Where the design

has an obvious direction make sure that all pieces of the garment are cut in the same way.
▦ Pin the pattern pieces to the fabric at about 4in (10cm) intervals and cut out with sharp shears. Mark any pocket or button positions before removing the pattern pieces.

WORKING WITH DIFFICULT FABRICS

Knits
When stitching, use a fine synthetic thread and a ball-point machine needle. Sew with a slight zigzag stitch, which will give a little with the fabric.

Sheer fabrics
When cutting out, pin to a blanket or sheet to prevent the fabric from sliding about the cutting surface. Sew with a fine needle and synthetic thread; if necessary, stitch between layers of tissue paper. Stitch together with French seams and use double hems to avoid unsightly edges.

Velvet and corduroy
Place the pattern pieces so the pile runs up on the finished garment. Stitch together in the direction of the pile, using tissue paper if necessary. Avoid buttonholes; use button loops instead or zippers, which should be inserted by hand with tiny back stitches. When pressing place a piece of self-fabric over or under the fabric to prevent the pile from flattening.

Vinyl
Hold the pattern pieces in position with adhesive tape. Use the same method when holding pieces together for stitching. When stitching, use a roller foot to help feed the fabric through the machine. Do not press vinyl with an iron.

Fur fabrics
Place the pattern pieces on single thickness of fabric, pile side down; cut so that the pile runs down the garment. On knit-backed fur fabric stitch with a slight zigzag stitch. After stitching

shave the pile from the seam allowances and tease out the pile from the stitched seams.

SEAMS AND STITCHES

Plain seam
Place the two fabric pieces with right sides together, raw edges even; pin and stitch together ⅝in (1.5cm) from the raw edges. Work a few stitches in reverse at each end of the seam to secure the threads.
▦ The simplest method of finishing the seam allowance edges is by machine zigzag stitching. Use a short, narrow stitch worked slightly in from the raw edge. If the fabric has a tendency to fray use a larger stitch and work over the raw edge.
▦ Where the fabric is fine turn under the raw edge and either zigzag stitch or stitch with a straight stitch.
▦ If you are finishing by hand overcast the raw edges: work from left to right (or vice versa, if you are left-handed), taking the thread diagonally over the edge and keeping the stitches about ⅛in (3mm) apart.
If the fabric tends to fray work a row of straight stitching first, then overcast the edge. If the fabric is heavy simply pink the edges using a pair of pinking shears.

French seam
A self-finishing seam used mainly on sheer and lightweight fabrics. Place the two fabric pieces with wrong sides together; pin and stitch ⅜in (1cm) from the raw edges. Trim and press the seam open. Refold with right sides together; pin and stitch ¼in (6mm) from the seamed edge.

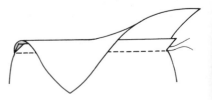

Flat fell seam

A self-finishing seam, which is very strong and distinctive. Place the two pieces with right sides together; pin and stitch a plain seam. Press seam allowances to one side. Trim down the lower seam allowance to ¼in (6mm). Fold the upper seam allowance over, enclosing the lower seam allowance. Press the folded allowance flat against the fabric; pin and stitch close to the folded edge.

Slipstitching

This hand stitch is used to join two folded edges – for example, to close an opening.

Bring the needle into one fold and come out ⅛in (2-3mm) further along; take a stitch the same length through the opposite fold. Pull the thread through and repeat. The stitches should be almost invisible.

Buttonhole stitch

Work the stitches close together, with the raw edge away from you. Insert the needle through the fabric ¼in (6mm) from the edge over the working thread; when the needle is pulled through a tiny loop is formed at the buttonhole edge. Do not pull the stitches too tight or the edge will pucker.

Topstitching

Stitching worked from the right side of the garment to emphasize the seam. Buttonhole thread can be used to make the stitching heavier and more visible.

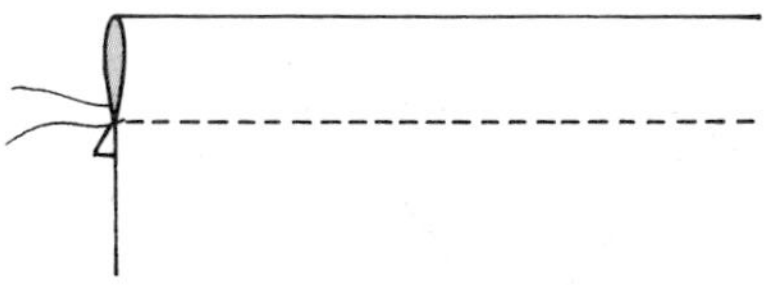

Hemming

Work this stitch with the hem away from you. After securing the working thread under the hem, take a tiny stitch through the main fabric – picking up one or two threads – and then a tiny stitch through the hem, then pull through; repeat, starting the next stitch directly below. The stitches should be about ¼in (6mm) apart.

Running stitch

This is the simplest of all the hand stitches. Weave the needle through the fabric at regular, short intervals. The spaces between the stitches are the same size as the stitches themselves. This stitch is most commonly used for gathering up fabrics.

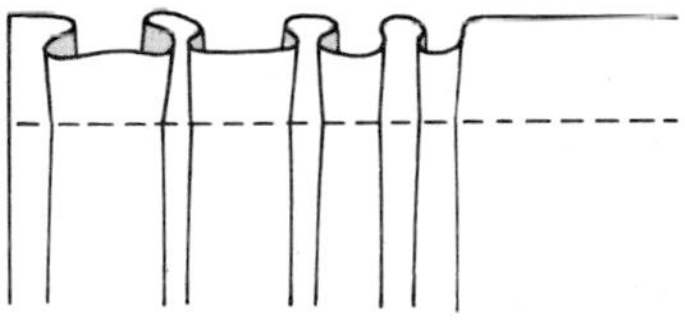

FASTENINGS

How to stitch on a button

At the marked position for the button, secure the thread on the right side of the fabric. Pass the needle through the button; hold a matchstick over the top of the button and work about 10 stitches over it through the holes of the button. Remove the matchstick and pull the button up; wind the working thread around the excess threads underneath button; work two backstitches into this shank and fasten off.

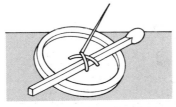

When the button itself has a shank, after securing the thread, take small stitches through the shank, again about 10 times. Fasten off.

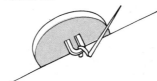

How to make a button loop

Mark the position of the loop on the fabric. Secure the thread on the wrong side of the fabric at one end of loop position. Bring thread through to right side and take a tiny stitch at the opposite end, leaving a loop of thread the correct size. Take thread back to starting point, leaving a second loop. Make two more loops in the same way and then buttonhole stitch over the loops. Fasten off.

Stitched buttonholes

Tack all around the buttonhole position and then cut along the marked line through all layers. Either using buttonhole thread or an ordinary sewing thread, secure the thread and begin at the inside edge of the garment. Work along the slit in buttonhole stitch, fanning out the stitches at the outside edge. Continue along the opposite side and then work a straight bar of stitches on the inside edge. Fasten off.

When working vertical buttonholes, work a bar at both ends.

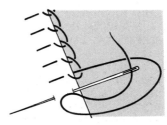

No-sew snaps

There are several types available: those held in place by pronged rings and those applied with a special tool. In each case there are two parts to each section, which are fastened in place on either side of the fabric. Plain or

decorative heads are available.

As an alternative to snap fasteners, there are nylon closure spots – small disks of nylon hooks and loops that cling together when pressed. Stitch these disks in place.

Sew-on snaps

Separate the two halves of the snap fastener. The ball half is sewn to the overlapping fabric, the socket half to the underlap.

Position the ball part on the fabric, at least ⅛in (3mm) from the edge. Secure the thread and work five or six stitches in each hole of the fastener, taking the needle under the fastener to the next hole each time. Fasten off the thread. Mark the position of the socket half opposite to it and stitch in place in the same way.

How to stitch on hooks and eyes

Stitch the hook to the overlap and the eye or bar to the underlap. After securing the thread, hold the hook firmly and work five to six stitches round the first loop, take the needle through the fabric to the next loop and repeat; then take the needle through the fabric to the end of the hook and work several stitches over the hook. Fasten off the thread. Stitch the eye or bar in place by stitching through the loops in the same way.

How to insert a zipper

Pin and stitch the seam up to the zipper opening, then tack the remainder of the seam. Press the seam open. Place the zipper face downwards over the seam allowances with the bottom stop ⅛in (3mm) below the beginning of the tacking and the teeth centered over the tacked seam. Tack in place through all layers ¼in (6mm) on either side of the teeth. Turn to the right side. Stitch the zipper in place using a zipper foot on the machine, following tacking lines at the sides, and pivoting the stitching at the bottom corners.

BABY BLUE BLOOMERS

A nautical stripe gives these beach bloomers great style. Elastic threaded at waist and ankles keeps sand and dirt out and they are stitched with French seams for a firm, tidy finish. The little shirt matches in spick-and-span fine stripes. Choose a soft, light seersucker fabric for coolness.

Size: to fit a one-year-old baby.

MATERIALS

BLOOMERS	SHIRT
⅝yd (50cm) of 36in (90cm) wide seersucker	1yd (1m) of 36in (90cm) wide seersucker
⅝yd (50cm) of 1in (2.5cm) wide elastic	¾yd (60cm) of 1in (2.5cm) wide self-fabric binding cut on the fabric bias
⅝yd (50cm) of ⅜in (1cm) wide elastic	Four ⅝in (1.5cm) diameter buttons
Two ⅝in (1.5cm) diameter buttons	Dressmakers' pattern paper
Dressmakers' pattern paper	Matching thread
Matching thread	

DIRECTIONS FOR BLOOMERS

▦ Draw up patterns from diagrams. Cut out following cutting instructions.

▦ Place fronts together; pin and stitch center front with French seam. Repeat with backs. Place front to back; pin and stitch sides and inner legs with French seams.

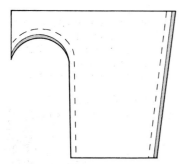

▦ Pin and stitch short ends of waistband together to form a ring. Place one edge of waistband to bloomer top with right sides together; pin and stitch. Fold waistband in half, then turn under remaining raw edge; pin and stitch, leaving an opening at center back seam.

▦ Thread wider elastic through the waistband; overlap ends for ⅜in (1cm) and stitch together. Push elastic into waistband and stitch up opening. Work two rows of stitching around the waistband over the elastic, evenly spacing rows about ¼in (6mm) apart.

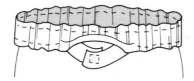

▦ Fold each strap in half lengthwise with right sides together; pin and stitch the long side, leaving a center opening. Refold with seam to center and stitch across both ends. Trim and turn to right side; slipstitch center opening to close.

▦ Place straps to right side of pants back 1¼in (3cm) from center back seam; pin and stitch in place. Work two vertical buttonholes on opposite ends of straps. Sew two buttons to inside of the waistband on either side of center front.

▦ Turn up a ⅝in (1.5cm) casing at the base of each leg, then tuck under ¼in (6mm); pin and stitch, leaving an opening at a seam. Stitch all around lower edge of casing. Thread elastic through casing; overlap ends for ⅜in (1cm) and stitch together. Push elastic into casing and stitch up opening.

for a day at the seaside

DIRECTIONS FOR SHIRT

▧ Draw up patterns from diagrams. Cut out following cutting instructions.

▧ Place backs to front; pin and stitch together at shoulders and sides with French seams.

▧ Fold sleeves in half; pin and stitch with French seams. Pin sleeves in armholes, matching side seams; stitch with French seams. Turn up a double 1¼in (3cm) hem along base of each sleeve; pin and stitch.

▧ Turn in center back edges along marked line. Open out one folded edge of bias binding and, with right sides together, place along seamline of neck edge; pin and stitch along fold line of binding. Press binding to the inside; pin and slipstitch in place.

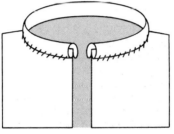

▧ Turn up lower edge of shirt for 1in (2.5cm), then tuck under ¼in (6mm); pin and hem.

▧ Work four horizontal buttonholes evenly spaced down right back, placing top buttonhole at neck edge. Stitch buttons to left back to correspond with buttonholes.

9

Pattern for bloomers

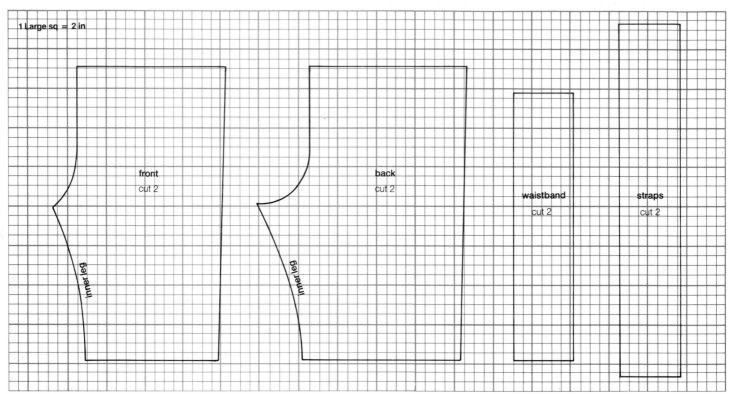

Pattern for shirt

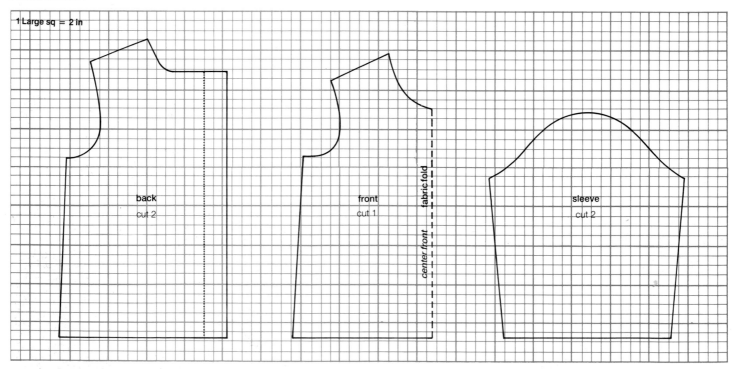

JAPANESE STYLE

High-fashion floral fabric makes a kimono-style jacket that fits easily over a wool jumper. The jacket is padded to keep baby snug and lined in a firm striped fabric to match the little pants. Cut out the kimono front and back with a big splash of flower in the center of the panels for the best decorative effect.

Size: to fit a nine-month-old baby.

MATERIALS

For jacket and pants.
1¼yd (1.2m) of 36in (90cm) wide large floral cotton fabric
2⅛yd (2m) of 36in (90cm) wide striped cotton fabric

¾yd (70cm) of 36in (90cm) wide
4oz (114gm) wadding
½yd (40cm) of ½in (1.2cm) wide elastic
Six snaps

DIRECTIONS FOR JACKET

▦ Draw up patterns from diagrams. Cut out following cutting instructions.

▦ Pin and stitch the floral jacket together at shoulder and side/underarm seams. Repeat with the striped jacket, then with the wadding.

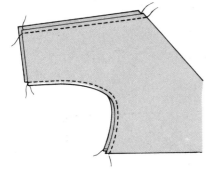

▦ With right sides together, place facing to striped jacket back neckline; pin and stitch round neckline. Stitch shoulder seams. Repeat with wadding.

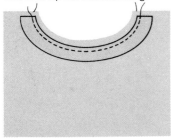

▦ Place the wadded jacket to wrong side of striped jacket; tack in place.

▦ With right sides together place floral jacket to striped jacket; pin and stitch left front edges from A round the base to right front at B. Trim and turn to right side. Topstitch round the outline of the larger flowers, working through all three layers.

▦ Place collar facing over edge of floral jacket, turn under seam allowance; pin and topstitch in place, trimming away excess wadding if necessary.

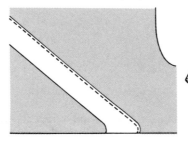

▦ Turn sleeve facing on to floral side of jacket, turn under seam allowance; pin and hem in place by hand.

▦ For ties, cut six pieces of striped fabric on the straight, 10¼in × 1in (26cm × 2.5cm).

▦ Fold ties in half lengthwise with right sides together; pin and stitch across one end and down length, taking a ¼in (6mm) seam allowance. Trim and turn to right side. Turn in raw edges at open end; slipstitch to close.

▦ Handstitch ties to floral side of jacket at B, C, D and E and to striped side of jacket at F and G.

DIRECTIONS FOR PANTS

▦ Place pants with right sides together; pin and stitch center seams.

▦ Turn down ¾in (2cm) at top edge, then tuck under ¼in (6mm), pin and stitch in place close to hem edge. Work a second line of stitching close to top edge of trousers, leaving an opening at one seam.

▦ Insert elastic round waist; overlap ends for ⅜in (1cm) and stitch together. Push elastic into waistband and stitch up opening.

▦ Turn a narrow double hem round inner leg seams. Attach no-sew fasteners in place, evenly spaced round the opening.

▦ Turn up hem on base of each pant leg for 1in (2.5cm), then tuck under ¼in (6mm); pin and hem in place by hand.

The large flowers on the cross-over jacket are emphasized with topstitching and team up with no-sew snap-closed pants.

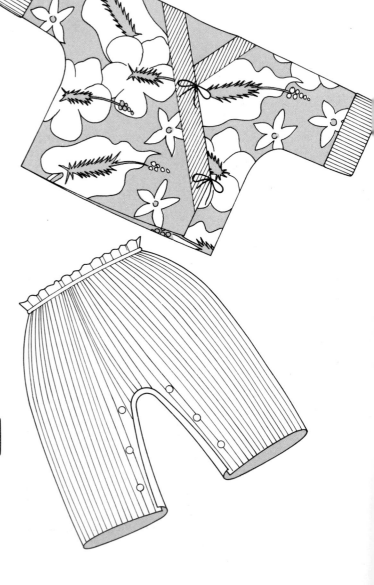

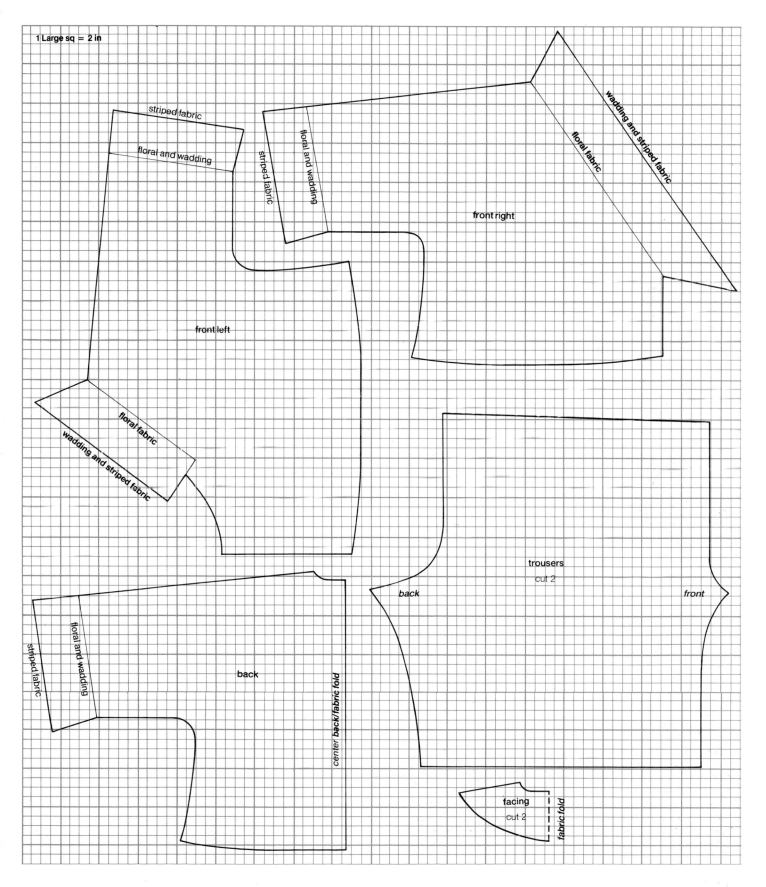

1 Large sq = 2 in

striped fabric

floral and wadding

striped fabric

floral and wadding

wadding and striped fabric

floral fabric

front right

front left

floral fabric

wadding and striped fabric

trousers
cut 2

back

front

striped fabric

floral and wadding

back

center back/fabric fold

facing
cut 2

fabric fold

FANCY JUMPSUIT

There's no need for jumpsuits to be strictly utilitarian. Make a feature of their loose fit with a design reminiscent of a clown's jumpsuit. The pretty stepped cut-out is easy to sew and simply fastened in place with Velcro spots. Use contrast colors with all the magic of the ring: red and yellow, blue and white, green and sizzling pink.

Size: to fit an eighteen-month-old baby

MATERIALS

⅞yd (80cm) of 55in (140cm) wide red brushed jersey	Two stretch waistbands: one red, one yellow
½yd (40cm) of 55in (140cm) wide yellow brushed jersey	Nylon closure spots (Velcro)
Two sets of stretch cuffs: one red, one yellow	Dressmakers' pattern paper
	Matching thread

DIRECTIONS

▦ Draw up patterns from diagrams. Cut out following cutting instructions.

▦ Place red backs with right sides together; pin and stitch center back seam.

▦ Fold under seam allowance on yellow back, then place over seam allowance on red back; pin and topstitch in place.

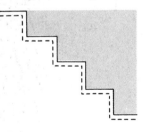

section to correspond with those on red facing.

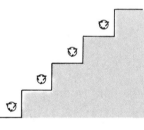

▦ Place sleeves together in pairs – red to yellow with right sides together; pin and stitch center seams. Position sleeves to body sections; pin and stitch in place.

▦ Pin and stitch side seams from wrist along underarm seams to ankles, catching edges of facings in the seam.

▦ With right sides together, zigzag stitch stretch cuffs to sleeve bases, slightly stretching the ribbed cuff as you sew. Repeat for ankle bands.

▦ Place the red fronts with right sides together; pin and stitch center front seam. Place red front facings with right sides together; pin and stitch. Snip corners. Turn facing to inside and topstitch. Edge-finish base of facing. Stitch nylon closure spots to facing.

▦ Edge-finish lower edge of yellow front upper left section. Stitch opposite halves of nylon closure spots to yellow front

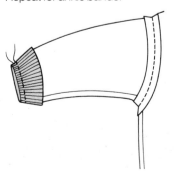

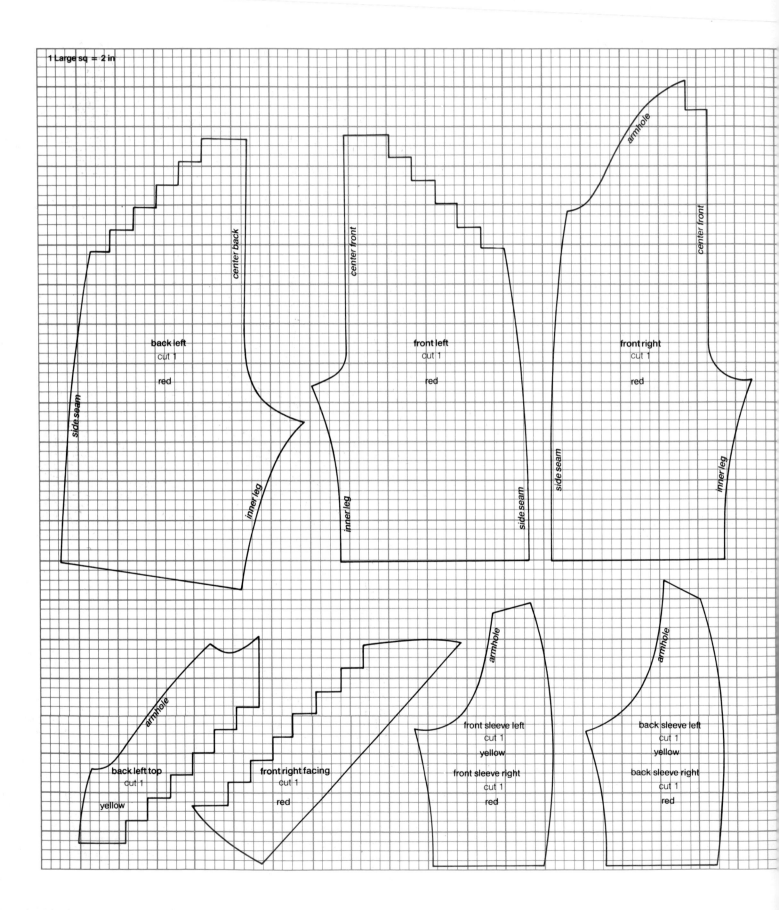

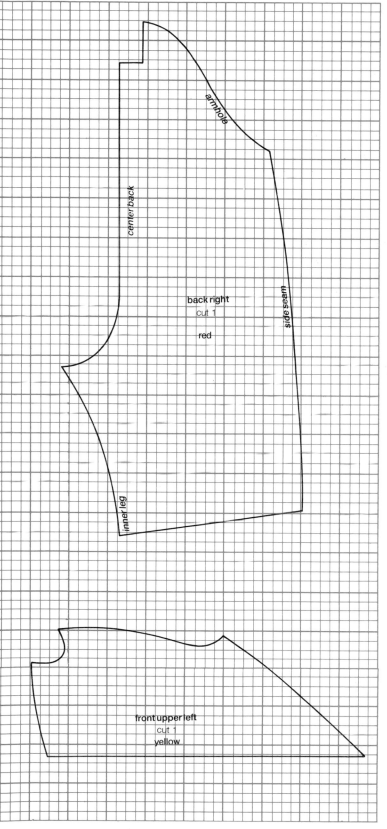

back right
cut 1

red

center back

armhole

side seam

inner leg

front upper left
cut 1
yellow

▨ For collar cut one piece from red waistband 3½in × 3¼in (9cm × 8cm) for right collar, and one piece from yellow waistband 9in × 3¼in (23cm × 8cm) for left collar.

▨ With right sides facing, pin and stitch collars together. Fold collar in half lengthwise with right sides together; pin and stitch ends. Turn to right side and stitch to neck edge, slightly stretching as you sew. Fasten at neck with one nylon closure spot.

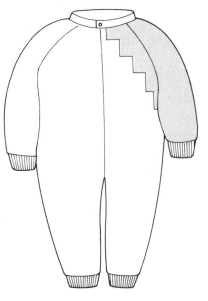

The zigzagged front hides a row of nylon closure spots, while the wrists and ankles are finished with stretch fabric bands.

17

ALL-IN-ONE SUITS

Forget the workaday overall image – these new designs are much more fun and they are ideal for all sorts of activities.

Make the indoor version in a glowing cotton chintz that is irresistible for lounging in or can be worn at bedtime in place of a dowdy old bathrobe. The outdoor version in a windproof fabric will fit over the chunkiest knit, and has big patch pockets to hide little secrets. Elastic and a strong front zipper keep wet and wind out.

Size: to fit a two-year-old.

MATERIALS

1⅝yd (1.5m) of 45in (112/114cm) wide plain or printed cotton fabric 12in (30cm) zipper	12in (30cm) of elastic Dressmakers' pattern paper Matching thread

DIRECTIONS

▦ Draw up patterns from diagrams. Cut out following cutting instructions.

▦ Place backs with right sides together; pin and stitch center back seam. Repeat with front pieces, but only stitch seam from A to B. Edge-finish. Turn in seam allowance on either side of center front from A to neck edge; tack.

▦ Turn in ¼in (6mm) on top edge of each pocket; pin and stitch. Turn down the right side of each pocket top for ¾in (2cm); pin and stitch sides. Snip corners and turn hem to inside of pocket; topstitch across top edge. Turn under seam allowance all round outer edge of pocket; tack. Place pockets on fronts at marked positions; pin and topstitch.

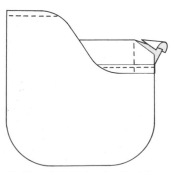

▦ Place front to back with right sides together; pin and stitch

shoulder, side and inner leg seams. Edge-finish. Turn up 1in (2.5cm) hem at base of each leg, then tuck under ¼in (6mm); pin and stitch hem.

▦ Fold sleeves in half with right sides together; pin and stitch seams. Pin sleeves in armholes with right sides together, matching underarm seams; stitch. Edge-finish.

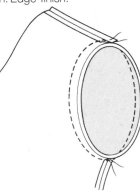

▦ At the base of each sleeve either turn up a 1in (2.5cm) hem then tuck under ¼in (6mm); pin and stitch hem.

▦ Or, for a gathered sleeve, pin and stitch a casing, leaving an opening at seam. Using a safety pin, thread elastic through the casing from opening in the seam; overlap ends of elastic for ⅜in (1cm) and stitch together firmly. Push elastic into casing and stitch up opening by hand or machine.

for indoors and outdoors

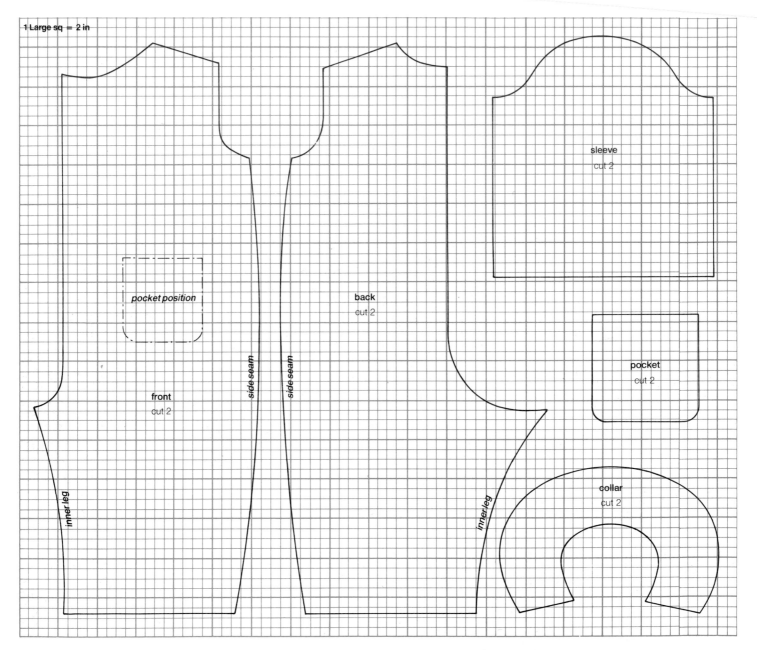

1 Large sq = 2 in

sleeve
cut 2

pocket position

back
cut 2

side seam

side seam

front
cut 2

pocket
cut 2

inner leg

inner leg

collar
cut 2

▦ If closing the center front with a zipper, insert now, before adding the collar.

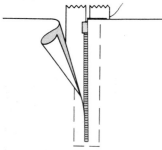

▦ Place collars with right sides together; pin and stitch all round outer edge, leaving neck edge open. Trim and turn to right side.
▦ Place facing neck edge of collar to neck edge of suit with right sides together, matching collar edges to folded front edges; pin and stitch.

▦ Turn under remaining raw edge and slipstitch over previous stitches. Topstitch around collar, ¼in (6mm) from outer edge.
▦ If closing the center front with ties, make up four pairs of 8in × ⅜in (20cm × 1cm) long ties: cut eight pieces of fabric on the bias, each 8¼in × 1¼in (21cm × 3.5cm). Fold each in half lengthwise with right sides together; pin and stitch across one end and down the length taking ¼in (6mm) seam allowance. Trim and turn to right side. Turn in raw edges and

sew on in pairs evenly spaced from neck edge down the center.

Outdoors, a neat zipper fastens this all-in-one suit against the cold, while indoors self-fabric ties make a decorative fastening.

BORN IN AN ORCHARD

On hot summer days, little kids need comfy and loosely fitting clothes for running about. These clever playsuits are roomy with eye-catching detail at the shoulders. For little girls and boys, make delectable strawberry trims for the pants shoulder straps, and sweet cherry ties on the sleeved suit. Note the French perfection of tucks on the cuffs to match the fronts – that's summer chic!

Sizes: to fit a three- or four-year-old.

MATERIALS

PAJAMAS
1⅞yd (1.7m) of 36in (90cm) wide green poplin
1⅝yd (1.5m) of 1in (2.5cm) wide red bias binding
Dressmakers' pattern paper
Four strawberry motifs
Matching thread

COMBINATION SUIT
2⅛yd (2m) of 36in (90cm) wide acid green or pink poplin
2⅛yd (2m) of 1in (2.5cm) wide bias binding, in matching colors
1⅜yd (1.2m) of ½in (1.3cm) wide bias binding
Dressmakers' pattern paper
Eight cherry motifs
Matching thread

DIRECTIONS FOR MOTIFS

STRAWBERRIES

▦ Cut out two strawberry shapes from fabric.

▦ Using ecru embroidery cotton, work a few evenly spaced running stitches on the right side of each shape for seeds.

▦ Place with right sides together; pin and stitch together close to outer edge, leaving a small opening at the top. Turn to right side. Fill with suitable filling and slip stitch opening.

▦ Cut out two leaves from fabric in different shades of green. Fix one leaf on top of the other.

CHERRIES

▦ Cut out a 2½in (6.5cm) diameter circle from fabric.

▦ Turn in a narrow hem all round the edge. Work a gathering stitch close to hemmed outer edge. Fill with suitable filling. Pull up gathering thread around filling and fasten off.

the pick of the bunch

DIRECTIONS FOR PAJAMAS

▦ Draw up pattern from diagram. Cut out following cutting instructions.

▦ Place back/front pieces with right sides together; pin and stitch center front and then center back seams, leaving 2¾in (7cm) open at top.

▦ Fold and pin eight ¾in (2cm) wide knife pleats along the top front so that they meet at center front, as shown in diagram. Fold and pin four ¾in (2cm) wide knife pleats along each back section in the same way. Using red thread, topstitch down the fold edge of each pleat for 2½in (6cm).

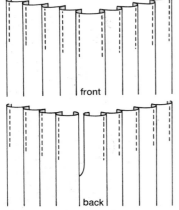

▦ Fold and pin eight ¾in (2cm) wide knife pleats around the base of each leg; topstitch up the fold edge of each pleat for 3¼in (8cm).

▦ Open out one folded edge of bias binding and, with right sides together, place along back opening; pin and stitch along fold line of binding. Press binding to the inside; pin and stitch in place.

▦ Fold bias binding in half lengthwise over raw edges of armholes, legs and neck edges, turning under raw edges at back opening; pin and stitch in place.

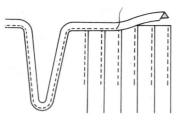

▦ Make up four ties each 8in × ⅜in (20cm × 1cm): cut four pieces of fabric on the bias, each 8¼in × 1¼in (21cm × 3.5cm). Fold each in half lengthwise with right sides together; pin and stitch across one end and down the length, taking a ¼in (6mm) seam allowance. Trim and turn to right side. Turn in raw edges at open end and slipstitch, then place, inside the garment, in pairs at the end of the outer front and back pleats; pin and handstitch in place. Stitch a strawberry motif to the end of each tie.

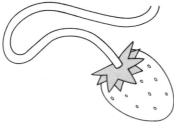

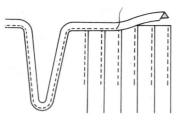

center back

back and front
cut 2

center front

inner leg

inner leg

1 Large sq = 4 in

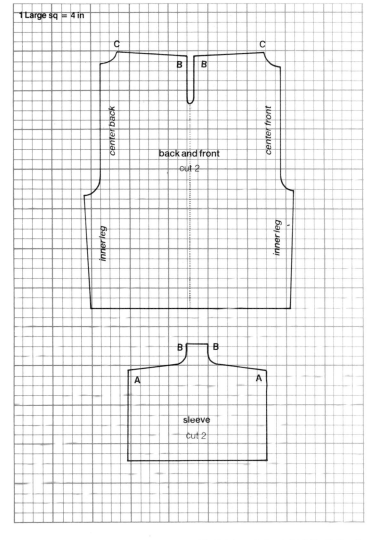

1 Large sq = 4 in

C   B   B   C

center back   center front

back and front
cut 2

inner leg   inner leg

B   B

A   A

sleeve
cut 2

DIRECTIONS FOR COMBINATION SUIT

▦ Draw up patterns from diagrams. Cut out following cutting instructions.

▦ Fold and pin four ⅝in (1.5cm) wide knife pleats on each back and front shoulder, as shown in the diagram. Using contrasting thread, topstitch down the fold edge of each pleat for 2½in (6cm).

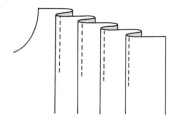

▦ Fold and pin eight ⅝in (1.5cm) wide knife pleats around the base of each sleeve. Using contrasting thread, topstitch up the fold edge of each pleat for 1½in (4cm).

▦ Fold and pin eight ¾in (2cm) wide knife pleats around the base of each leg. Using contrasting thread, topstitch up the fold edge of each pleat for 2½in (6cm).

▦ Place back/front pieces with right sides together; pin and stitch center back and then center front seam for 3¼in (8cm). Pin and stitch inner leg seams.

▦ Fold sleeves in half with right sides together; pin and stitch seams. Pin sleeves in armholes with right sides together, matching the As, Bs and Cs; stitch. Press the seams flat towards the sleeve; topstitch

seams in contrasting thread.

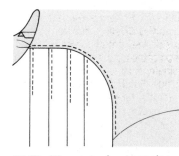

▦ Bind the center front opening, sleeves, legs and neck edge with bias binding in the same way as for the pajamas.

▦ For the ties, cut eight 6in (15cm) lengths from ½in (1.3cm)

wide binding. Fold in half lengthwise; pin and stitch down length, then tuck in raw edges at each end. Stitch ties in pairs behind front opening, spacing them 3½in (9cm) apart, with top pair at neck edge. Stitch a cherry motif to the end of each tie.

BEDTIME FUN

Three stunning outfits in cuddly brushed cotton give you sing-song colors and easy-to-sew shapes. There's a design to please every personality: 'Jump for Joy', a sleepsuit with a pierrot collar for the irrepressible; 'Harlequin', a mini-bathrobe for the man about the house, and 'Red at Night', a glamour gown with a hood and pompoms. Don't forget the Bugs Bunny bootees, which will be a joy to all parties: they're made to match each outfit.

Sizes: to fit a two-year-old.

MATERIALS

BOOTEES
4in (10cm) of 36in (90cm) wide brushed cotton
20in (50cm) of bias binding in a matching color
6in (15cm) square of non-slip material
Fabric glue

One 2oz (50g) ball of Pingouin Pingofine
Pair of size 1 (2¾mm) knitting needles
Two mother-of-pearl buttons, for eyes
Black embroidery cotton, for features
Matching thread

HARLEQUIN
1½yd (1.4m) of 36in (90cm) wide brushed cotton

1yd (1m) of cord in contrasting color
Matching thread

RED AT NIGHT
1⅛yd (1.1m) of 36in (90cm) wide brushed cotton
3¼yd (3m) of ¾in (2cm) wide braid

Matching thread
Scraps of yarn in three colors to match braid

JUMP FOR JOY
1¾yd (1.6m) of 36in (90cm) wide blue brushed cotton
½yd (40cm) of 36in (90cm) wide pink brushed cotton
One 2oz (50g) ball of Pingouin Pingofrance

Pair of size 4 (3¾mm) knitting needles
Piece of ½in (1.3cm) wide elastic
Two small buttons
Piece of bias binding
Small amount of filling
Matching thread

HOW TO MAKE A POMPOM
Cut two circles of cardboard to the required diameter of the pompom. Cut a small circle from the center of each one. Place the disks together and wind yarn round and round them. When the center gets full, thread the yarn on a bodkin and 'sew' through the hole until it is filled. Cut through the loops at the outer edge and pull the pieces of card slightly apart. Tie a short length of yarn firmly round the loops between the two disks. Then pull the disks away and fluff out the finished pompom.

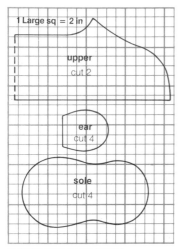

DIRECTIONS FOR BOOTEES

▦ Draw up patterns from diagrams. Cut out following cutting instructions.

▦ Place soles together in pairs with wrong sides together, matching outer edges; pin and zigzag stitch together all round.

▦ Fold each upper in half with right sides together; pin and stitch center front seam. Place each upper to a combined sole with right sides together, matching center front seam to sole front and center back fold to sole back; pin and zigzag stitch together all round.

▦ Fold bias binding in half lengthwise over zigzagged edges of sole. Turn under raw edge of binding and overlap at center back to finish; pin and stitch binding in place.

▦ Place the bootee on the wrong side of the non-slip material and mark round it. Cut out two soles; glue to fabric soles. When the glue is dry, stitch around bootees again over bias binding.

▦ Place ears together in pairs with right sides facing; pin and stitch together all round, leaving base edge open. Trim and turn to right side.

▦ Make a face on each bootee with ears and button eyes, and add a nose in satin stitch and whiskers in long straight stitches.

▦ For each ankle band, cast on 60sts. Work in K1, P1 rib for 4in (10cm). Bind off. Fold in half and stitch seam. Stitch ankle band to top of bootee.

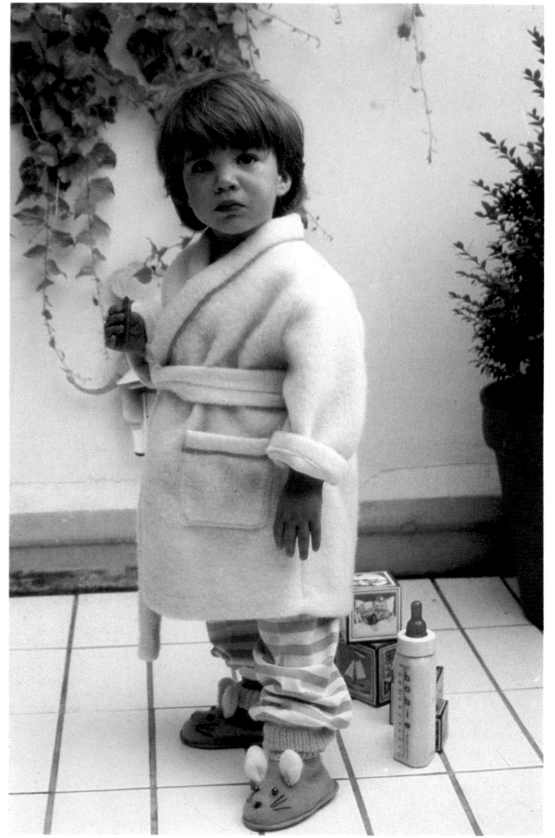

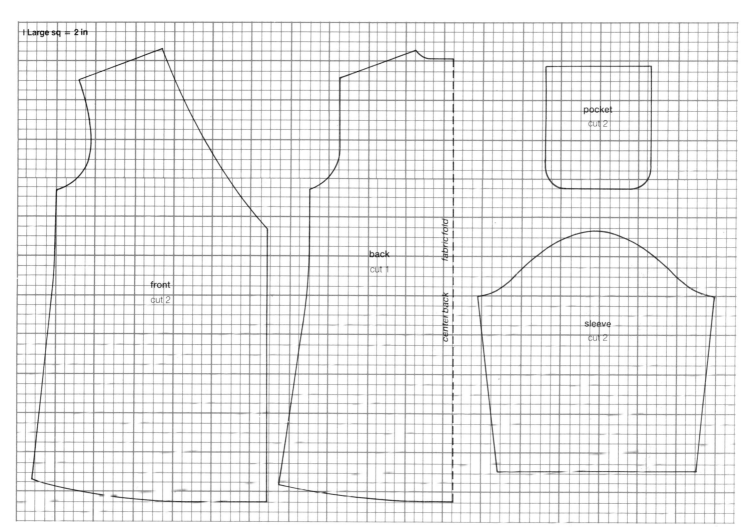

I Large sq = 2 in

pocket
cut 2

front
cut 2

back
cut 1

center back

fabric fold

sleeve
cut 2

DIRECTIONS FOR HARLEQUIN

▦ Draw up patterns from diagrams. Cut out following cutting instructions.

▦ From remaining fabric, cut out one collar strip 26in × 3in (65cm × 7.5cm) and one belt strip 54in × 4in (140cm × 10cm).

▦ With right sides together, pin and stitch fronts to back along side and shoulder seams.

▦ To make pocket facing, turn down right side of each pocket top for 1in (2.5cm); pin and stitch ends of facing. Snip corners and turn facing to wrong side of pocket; topstitch across pocket top ¾in (2cm) from edge.

▦ Handstitch cord across topstitching. Turn under remaining edges of pocket; pin and tack.

▦ Position pockets on fronts 2½in (6cm) from side seams and 8in (20cm) up from base edge; pin and topstitch in place.

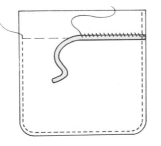

▦ Fold sleeves with right sides together; pin and stitch underarm seams.

▦ Pin sleeves in armholes with right sides together, matching center top of sleeve to shoulder seam and matching underarm seams together; stitch in place.

▦ Place collar to neck edge of bathrobe with right sides together; pin and stitch.

▦ Fold collar in half lengthwise with right sides together, overlapping long raw edge by ⅝in (1.5cm); pin and stitch ends. Edge-finish remaining raw edge; turn; stitch along seamline. Handstitch cord to bathrobe over seamline of collar on right side.

▦ Fold belt in half with right sides together; pin and stitch, leaving a central opening in long side. Trim and turn to right side; slipstitch central opening to close.

▦ To hold belt in place, work two loops slightly larger than belt width at each side seam.

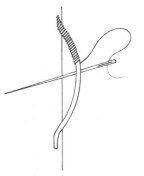

▦ Turn under 2½in (6cm) along base edge, then tuck under ¼in (6mm); pin and hem in place.

▦ Turn under 1in (2.5cm) along lower edge of each sleeve, then tuck under ¼in (6mm); pin and hem in place.

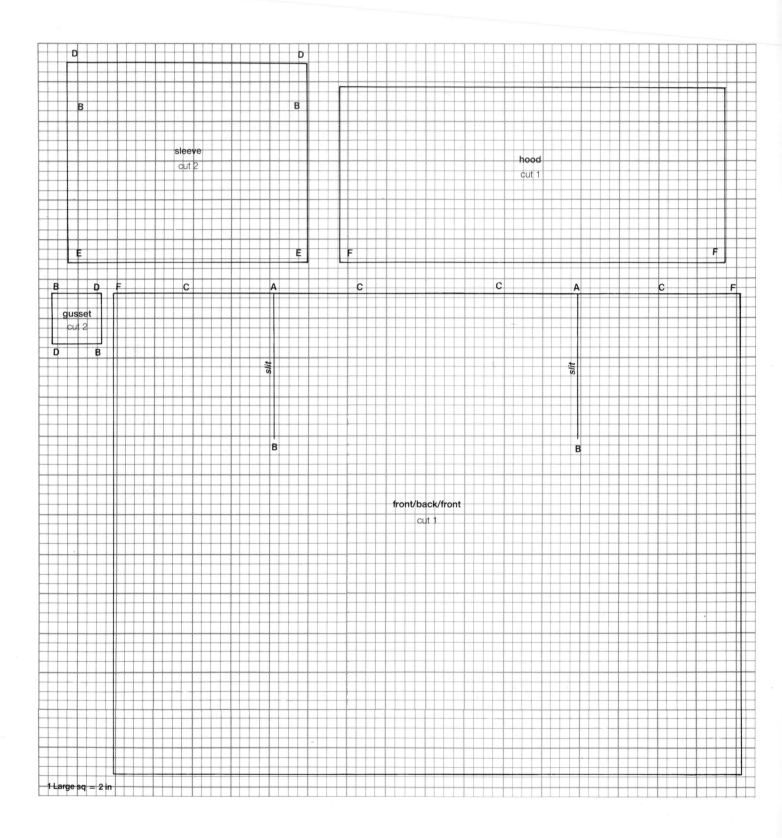

DIRECTIONS FOR RED AT NIGHT

▦ Draw up patterns from diagrams. Cut out following cutting instructions.

▦ To form armholes, cut down the combined front/back from A to B for 7in (18cm). Zigzag stitch raw edge of each armhole.

▦ Fold back and front with right sides together; pin and stitch shoulder seams A to C.

▦ Fold each gusset in half diagonally B to B. With right sides together, pin and stitch B/D side of gusset to B/D on each side of sleeve.

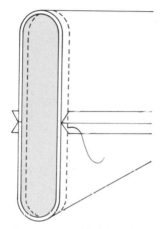

▦ Fold sleeves with right sides together. Pin D/D side of sleeve in armhole slits AB; stitch.

▦ With right sides together, pin and stitch hood to neck edge. Trim and press seam open. Center the braid over seam on wrong side covering raw edges; pin and topstitch in place.

▦ Fold braid in half lengthwise over raw front edges; pin and topstitch in place. Overlap front braids and stitch center front seam, leaving 6in (15cm) open at both top and bottom of seam.

▦ Turn under 2½in (6cm) along base edge, then tuck under ¼in (6mm); pin and hem in place. Repeat for each sleeve, but make a 1in (2.5cm) hem.

▦ Make a pompom from each yarn color; stitch pompoms in place down center front seam.

DIRECTIONS FOR JUMP FOR JOY

▦ Draw up patterns from diagrams. Cut out following cutting instructions.

▦ From remaining pink fabric, cut out two 2in (5cm) diameter circles for pompoms.

▦ Place upper backs to front with right sides together; pin and stitch side seams from D to C.

▦ With right sides together, place lower backs to front, overlapping upper back pieces; pin and stitch side seams from E to D, continuing stitching through three thicknesses at D for about ³⁄₈in (1cm). Edge-finish side seams and top edge of flap.

▦ Turn a ⁵⁄₈in (1.5cm) hem along side edges of back flap; pin and stitch. Turn under a ³⁄₄in (2cm) hem along top edge of back flap; pin and stitch. Push a length of elastic through back casing and stitch at each end to hold. Work a horizontal buttonhole at each end of back casing.

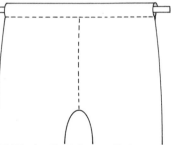

▦ Work a tight zigzag stitch around curved edge of upper back. Stitch a button to edges of upper back to match buttonholes.

▦ With right sides together, pin and stitch inner leg seams.

▦ Fold sleeve with right sides together; pin and stitch side seams. Pin sleeves in armholes with right sides together, matching AC and BC; stitch in place.

▦ Work buttonhole stitch all round outer edge of collar.

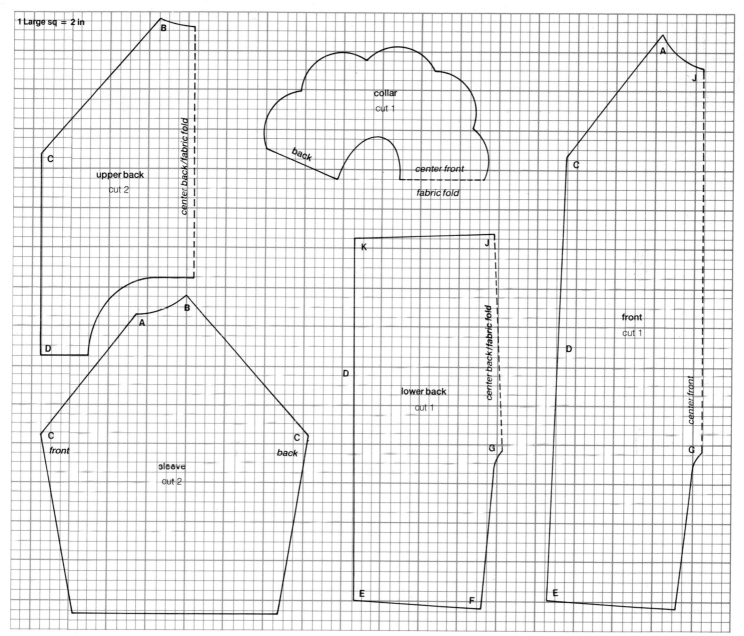

1 Large sq = 2 in

collar
cut 1

back

center front

fabric fold

center back / fabric fold

upper back
cut 2

C

B

D

A

B

C front

C back

sleeve
cut 2

K

J

D

center back / fabric fold

lower back
cut 1

G

E

F

A

J

C

front
cut 1

D

center front

G

E

◫ Place collar to neck edge with right side of collar to wrong side of neck edge; pin and stitch in place. To finish the inside edge, fold bias binding over raw edges; pin and stitch in place. Fold collar over to right side of jump suit.

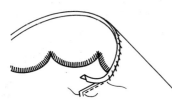

◫ Run a line of gathering stitches round each pompom circle. Pull up gathering stitches round a small amount of filling; fasten. Stitch pompoms in place on front of jump suit.

◫ Work a row of gathering stitches round ends of sleeves and legs.

◫ For each cuff, cast on 40 sts. Work in K1, P1 rib for 2in (5cm).

Bind off. Stitch side seam of each cuff.

◫ For each ankle band, cast on 50 sts. Work in K1, P1 rib for 3½in (9cm). Bind off. Stitch side seam of each band.

◫ Place a knitted cuff to end of each sleeve; pin and stitch in place, pulling up gathering evenly to fit. Stitch ankle bands to base of each trouser leg in the same way.

ONE YEAR OLD ALREADY

A first birthday is a big moment and baby deserves a fancy outfit for the celebration. Boys can wear ribbons too, just like girls – stitched in a smart pattern to make one side of a reversible quilted jacket. The ribbon fabric is made up first and then stitched to the floral lining with a light layer of wadding between for warmth.

Size: to fit a nine- to twelve-month-old baby.

MATERIALS

PANTS
⅝yd (50cm) of 45in (114cm) wide floral cotton drapery fabric
¾yd (70cm) of 3¼in (8cm) wide ribbon
½yd (40cm) of ⅝in (1.5cm) wide elastic
Dressmakers' pattern paper
Matching thread

JACKET
¾yd (60cm) of 45in (114cm) wide floral drapery fabric
¾yd (60cm) of 45in (114cm) wide curtain lining
¾yd (60cm) of 36in (90cm) wide wadding
1yd (1m) of 6in (15cm) wide ribbon
3¼yd (3m) of 1½in (4cm) wide ribbon
2⅛yd (2m) of 1in (2.5cm) wide ribbon
2⅛yd (2m) of ⅝in (1.5cm) wide ribbon
1½yd (1.2m) of ¼in (6mm) wide green ribbon
¾yd (60cm) of ¼in (6mm) wide pink ribbon
Dressmakers' pattern paper
Dressmakers' carbon paper
Matching thread

DIRECTIONS FOR PANTS

▨ Draw pattern from diagram. Cut out following cutting instructions.

▨ Place a length of 3¼in (8cm) wide ribbon along base edge of each pant leg, with right sides together; pin and stitch around base of trousers, continuing stitching around both sides of marked slit. Cut slit and snip corners. Fold the ribbon down.

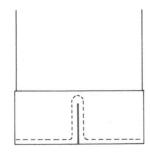

▨ Pin and stitch inner leg seams, with right sides together, continuing stitching through ribbon. Edge-finish and press open. Turn ribbon to the wrong side and handstitch in place.

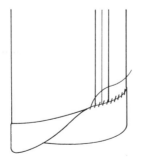

▨ With right sides together, pin and stitch pants pieces together from center front round to center back. Snip curved seam.

▨ Turn under top edge for 1in (2.5cm), tuck under ¼in (6mm); pin and stitch in place, leaving an opening at one seam. Thread elastic through the waist casing; overlap ends for ⅜in (1cm) and stitch together. Push elastic into casing and stitch up opening.

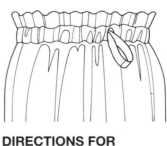

DIRECTIONS FOR JACKET

▨ Draw pattern from the diagram.
▨ Mark the outline of the pattern on the curtain lining, using dressmakers' carbon paper. Place the ribbons, right side up, on the lining, completely covering the outlined jacket pattern; pin and topstitch ribbons in place.

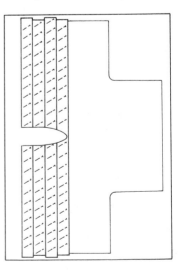

chintz and ribbons for a star turn

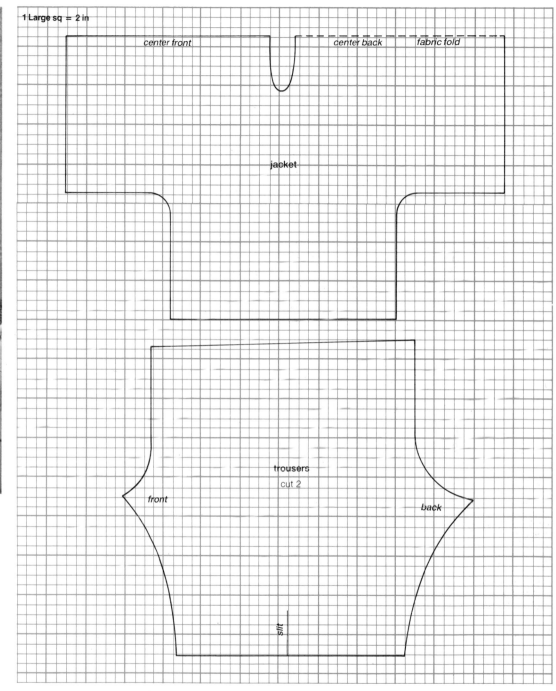

1 Large sq = 2 in

center front   center back   fabric fold

jacket

trousers
cut 2

front

back

slit

▥ Cut out one jacket in ribboned fabric, one in floral fabric and one in wadding. Tack the wadding to the wrong side of the floral print fabric. With right sides together, pin and stitch side/underarm seams on both jackets.

▥ With right sides together, place the wadded jacket to ribbon jacket; pin and stitch front edges and around neck edge. Trim and turn to right side.

▥ Turn in sleeve and jacket hems for ⅝in (1.5cm); pin and topstitch close to hem edge. Topstitch around neck edge and down front edges to match.

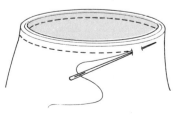

▥ Topstitch vertically down the jacket at 1½in (4cm) intervals.

▥ Cut ¼in (6mm) wide green ribbon into four equal pieces and cut ¼in (6mm) wide pink ribbon in half. Handstitch to jacket front, with top pair 1½in (4cm) down from neck edge and then at 4in (10cm) intervals, placing the pair of pink ribbons in the middle.

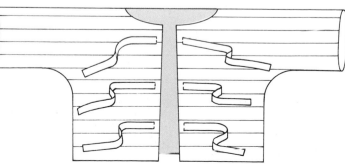

GOOD MORNING

If plain sewing gives you pleasure and time-consuming embroidery drives you to distraction, then these pink, painted cotton pajamas are perfect for you. A simple stand collar and patch pockets are easy details to machine stitch, while the handwork is reduced to six bold buttons for the front. Five beautiful motifs, based on French wooden toys, are given for you to paint on; an instant, colorful effect.

Size: to fit a three-year-old.

MATERIALS

2¼yd (2.2m) of 36in (90cm) wide pink cotton fabric	Eight ¾in (2cm) diameter buttons Matching thread

DIRECTIONS

▦ Draw up patterns from diagram. Cut out following cutting instructions.

▦ To make up patch pockets, turn under top edge of each pocket for ¼in (6mm); pin and stitch. Turn a ¾in (2cm) wide facing to right side; pin and stitch sides. Snip corners. Turn facing to the wrong side of pocket; topstitch across top. Turn under seam allowances on side edges of pocket and place on front at marked positions; pin and topstitch pocket sides.

▦ Place front to back with right sides together; pin and stitch shoulder seams. Trim and edge-finish. Place sleeves to front/back with right sides together; pin and stitch. Trim and edge-finish.

▦ Fold jacket with right sides together; pin and stitch side seams, continuing to stitch underarm seam to wrist. Trim and edge-finish.

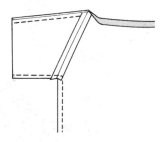

▦ Finish edges of front facings. Fold facings to the right side; pin and stitch top edges for 2⅝in (6.5cm). Fold facing to inside of jacket.

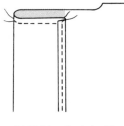

▦ Fold collar in half lengthwise with right sides together; pin and stitch ends. Trim and turn to the right side. Place one long edge of collar to right side of neck edge; pin and stitch. Trim and turn to inside. Turn under remaining edge of collar; pin and slipstitch in place.

▦ Mark and work four buttonholes down right-hand side of jacket. Stitch buttons to opposite side to match. Stitch buttons alongside buttonholes, to give a double-breasted effect.

▦ Turn up hem edge of jacket for ¾in (2cm), catching in base edges of pockets. Tuck under ¼in (6mm); pin and hem in place. Repeat for sleeve hems.

▦ Make up pants in the same way as pants on page 34.

HINTS FOR PAINTING MOTIFS

Before you start, mark the design on the fabric using dressmakers' carbon paper: trace off the design, place the tracing on the fabric in the correct place, slide a sheet of carbon paper between the tracing and the fabric, coated side down, and pin or hold firmly in place. Draw firmly over the lines of the design, then remove carbon and tracing. Pin the jacket on to a working board: over a layer of plastic and a layer of spare fabric. Try not to stretch the fabric as it will distort the motif.

▦ When working with fabric paints, use a soft dry brush, and rinse it well between each color change. Paints can also be mixed together to provide extra colors. Before you begin, test the paint colors on a spare piece of fabric, as some paint colors can alter when applied to strong-colored fabrics. Leave the fabric to dry, then fix the paint to the fabric by pressing with a very hot iron over a clean cotton cloth.

▦ Alternatively, use paint marker pens, which can produce very fine lines; however, they are not very good at filling in large areas of the same color as it is inclined to go streaky. As these pens are indelible the paint does not have to be fixed on to the fabric, but be careful, as any mistakes cannot be removed.

wooden toys to wake up with

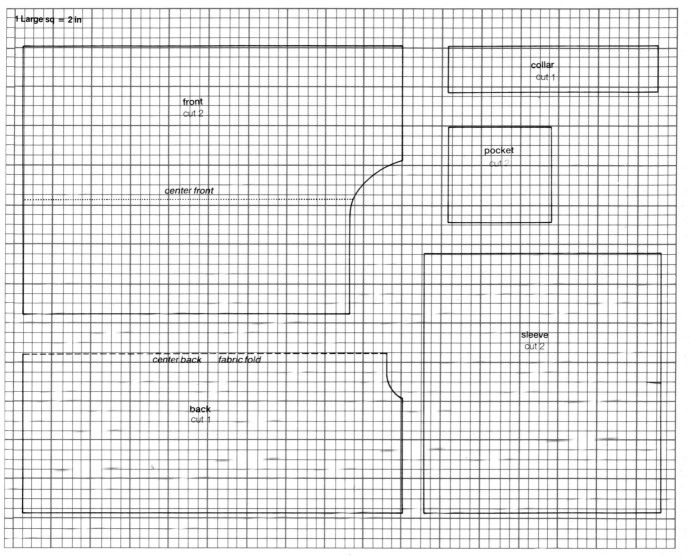

1 Large sq = 2 in

front
cut 2

center front

collar
cut 1

pocket
cut 2

sleeve
cut 2

center back   fabric fold

back
cut 1

Choose the motif designs for children's clothes from child-like objects and books. Enlist the child's help to pick the right one, as children have definite ideas about the clothes they want to wear. A good firm outline will be easy to fill in with paint on a fabric and bright colors will not only cheer up the garment but bring a touch of individuality and fun.

TUTTI FRUTTI

Delicious, delectable morsels – four pretty pinafores designed to melt the hardest heart. What better celebration of summer could there be? These fruity pinafores made of shiny chintz have straps criss-crossed at the back and stitched to a simple dirndl skirt. The padded shapes are quick to make, each one a perfect project for a holiday mood. Use the same idea for pants for a jealous brother.

Size: to fit a four-year-old.

MATERIALS

¾yd (70cm) of 48in (122cm) wide glazed cotton for skirt and straps	backing
	Dressmakers' pattern paper
Three ⅜in (1cm) diameter buttons	Embroidery cottons
Odds and ends of fabric and wadding for fruit motifs and	Dressmakers' carbon paper
	Matching thread

DIRECTIONS

To make basic skirt and straps.

▦ For the skirt cut one piece 48in × 17¾in (122cm × 45cm); a waistband 23in × 3½in (58cm × 9cm), and two straps each 48in × 2¾in (122cm × 7cm).

▦ Fold the skirt in half with right sides together. Pin and stitch, taking ⅝in (1.5cm) seam allowance, and leaving 6in (15cm) open at top. Turn in opening edges for ⅝in (1.5cm); pin.

▦ Work two rows of gathering stitches round top of skirt, ⅝in (1.5cm) from top raw edge. Pull up gathers evenly to 20⅝in (52cm) and stitch over the gathers to hold in place.

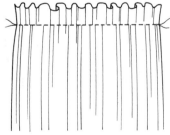

▦ Place waistband on skirt with right sides together, extending the band for 1¾in (4.5cm) at one side and ⅝in (1.5cm) at the other; and stitch. Fold band in half lengthwise with right sides together; pin and stitch ends and

along extensions. Refold with wrong sides together, turn under remaining raw edge and slipstitch over previous stitches.

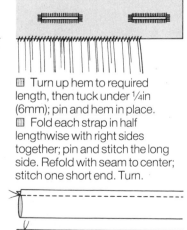

▦ Work a buttonhole on shorter waistband extension at center back and then one on either side 2½in (6cm) from the first buttonhole. Stitch a button to larger extension, to correspond with center back buttonhole.

▦ Turn up hem to required length, then tuck under ¼in (6mm); pin and hem in place.

▦ Fold each strap in half lengthwise with right sides together; pin and stitch the long side. Refold with seam to center; stitch one short end. Turn.

38

in four fabulous flavors

DIRECTIONS FOR WATER MELON

▦ Draw motif to size and mark the outline of the shape on a piece of white fabric, using dressmakers' carbon paper. Cut out, adding a 1¼in (3cm) margin all round.

▦ Using this as a pattern, cut out one shape from the wadding and one from pink fabric for backing.

▦ Place the white and pink fabrics with wrong sides together, sandwiching the wadding in between; tack.

▦ Mark and cut out the 'skin' from green fabric. Tack in place over marked outline. Mark and cut out pink 'flesh' and tack over outline.

▦ Zigzag stitch all round 'skin' and then 'flesh' with matching thread. Embroider 'pips' in dark brown embroidery cotton in satin stitch. Trim away excess fabric from around the motif.

DIRECTIONS FOR STRAWBERRY

▦ Draw motif to size and mark and cut out the shape, as above, from two layers of pink fabric and one layer of wadding, adding a 1¼in (3cm) margin all round.

▦ Place the fabrics with wrong sides together, sandwiching the wadding in between; tack. Zigzag stitch all round with matching pink thread.

▦ Mark and cut out leaf shape from green fabric. Place over strawberry, tack; then zigzag stitch in place, using matching green thread.

▦ Embroider French knots all over strawberry in yellow embroidery cotton. Trim away excess fabric around the motif.

DIRECTIONS FOR BANANA

▦ Draw motif to size. Mark and cut out the shape, as above, from two layers of yellow fabric and one layer of wadding, adding a 1¼in (3cm) margin all round.

▦ Place the fabrics with wrong sides together, sandwiching the wadding in between; tack.

▦ Zigzag stitch all round the outer edge and round the outline of each banana, using brown thread.

▦ Work the ridges in running stitch and the banana edges in stem stitch, using brown embroidery cotton. Trim away excess fabric around the motif.

Pick your favorite fruit and transform a dull skirt. Each fruit can be appliquéd in a variety of fabrics – try mixing and matching textures and embroidery cottons. There's no need to stick to nature's colors. Just choose the bright ones that children love to wear.

DIRECTIONS FOR PINEAPPLE

▨ Draw motif to size and mark and cut out the shape, as above, from two layers of yellow fabric and one layer of wadding, adding a 1¼in (3cm) margin all round.

▨ Place the fabrics with wrong sides together, sandwiching the wadding in between; tack.

▨ Stitch round the outline of the fruit using thread and zigzag round the outer edge in yellow.

▨ Mark and cut out the leaf from green fabric; tack to top of fruit.

▨ Zigzag stitch all round leaf using matching thread. Trim away excess fabric from around the motif.

TO COMPLETE PINAFORE

▨ For the strawberry, bananas and pineapple, center the motif on the front of the skirt; pin and handstitch in place at the back with invisible stitches.

▨ Place closed ends of straps behind the top of the fruit and stitch in place.

▨ Take the straps over the shoulders to cross over at the back. Mark positions of buttonholes.

▨ Trim off straps to required length, turn in raw edges and slipstitch. Stitch on buttons at marked positions.

▨ For water melon, pin and stitch straps to the front of the skirt behind the waistband, 2in (5cm) on either side of center front.

▨ Take straps over the shoulders and complete as before.

▨ Pin and handstitch water melon to straps at the front.

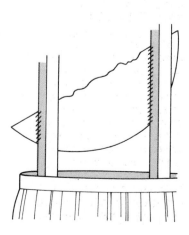

SMART STEPHANIE

Classic pleats like these have an ageless charm and suit all types, all ages. The dress is made of rectangles of fabric, pleated and tacked in place before it is sewn together.

Size to fit any size.

MATERIALS

To calculate the amount of material required, measure each section as described and allow for the length by three times the width measurement.

This will allow for the pleating. One ⅝in (1.5cm) button Matching thread

DIRECTIONS

Take the following measurements:
A – chest
B – neckline depth
C – total length of the dress
D – shoulder length
E – armhole length
F – width of back and front

▦ The main part of the dress is an oblong folded up into 1¼in (3cm) knife pleats; the width after pleating should be the same size as the chest A plus 1½in (4cm); the length should equal C.
▦ The straps that link the back to the front are two pleated oblongs: they measure, after pleating, the width of D by the length B.
▦ The sleeve frills are two pleated oblongs 3¼in (8cm) wide by the length E.

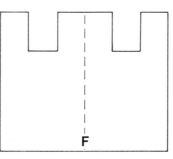

▦ Mark the center front of the main oblong. To make the armholes, cut rectangles out of the main part of the body parallel to the center front: the depth of the armhole equals E/B. For the width, take F away from A and divide the remainder by 4.

▦ To make up the dress, first pin and stitch the center back seam to within 6in (15cm) of the neck edge, taking a ⅝in (1.5cm) seam allowance. Trim and edge-finish.
▦ Work a button loop at the neck edge and add a button to fasten center back.
▦ Pin and stitch the straps in place. Pin and stitch sleeve frills in place.
▦ Turn up the lower edge of dress and sleeves to the required length; pin and hem in place.

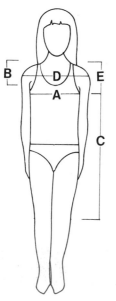

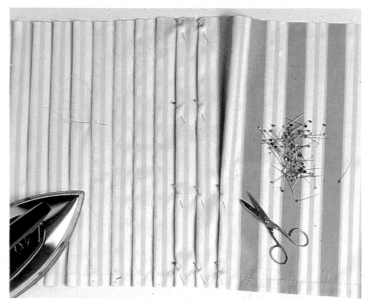

SHIPMATES

A smart sailor frock to see a girl through all childhood's adventures, even if they are only voyages in the unknown world of the imagination . . . Make them in wool, with mother-of-pearl buttons and satin or grosgrain ribbon, like they did in Edwardian days. The skirt is simply gathered on to a loose-fitting top that leaves enough room for a blouse, T-shirt or top underneath for winter warmth.

Size: to fit an eight- to ten-year-old.

MATERIALS

2⅛yd (1.9m) of 54/56in (140/150cm) wide wool mixture
6yd (5.5m) of ⅜in (1cm) wide white braid
¾yd (60cm) of 1in (2.5cm) wide white ribbon

Four ⅜in (1cm) mother-of-pearl buttons
Snap fastener
Dressmakers' pattern paper
Matching thread

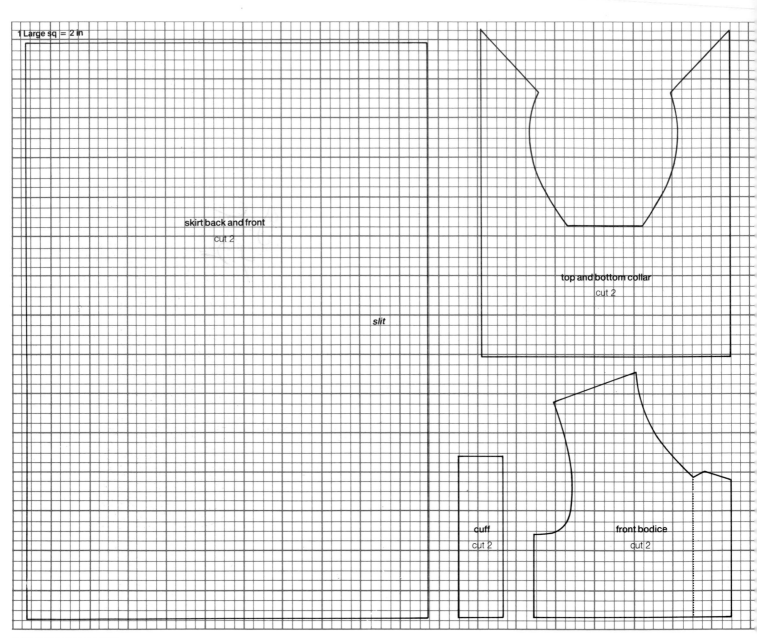

1 Large sq = 2 in

skirt back and front
cut 2

slit

top and bottom collar
cut 2

cuff
cut 2

front bodice
cut 2

DIRECTIONS FOR SAILOR DRESS

▥ Draw up patterns from diagrams. Cut out following cutting instructions.

▥ To make an opening, cut a 4in (10cm) long slit in the center front of the skirt, as marked on the pattern. Cut a straight strip of fabric 8in × 1¾in (20cm × 4.5cm). Pin strip down one side of slit and then up the second side, keeping right sides together; stitch close to edge. Fold the strip through center to wrong side. Turn under raw edge

for ⅛in (3mm); and slipstitch over previous stitching.

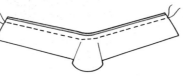

▥ Place skirt pieces with right sides together; pin and stitch side seams. Work two rows of gathering stitches ⅝in (1.5cm) from top of skirt. Pull up gathers evenly until skirt top measures 31½in (80cm); stitch over gathers to

hold in place.

▥ Place front bodice pieces to back bodice with right sides together; pin and stitch side and shoulder seams.

▥ Place skirt to bodice with right sides together, matching side seams and matching fold line of front bodice to edge of concealed front fastening; pin and stitch. Finish front edges of bodice; then fold front bodice edges to wrong side. Topstitch front opening close to edge from top to base.

▥ Fold sleeves with right sides together; pin and stitch underarm

seams. Work two rows of gathering stitches around top of each sleeve between A and B.

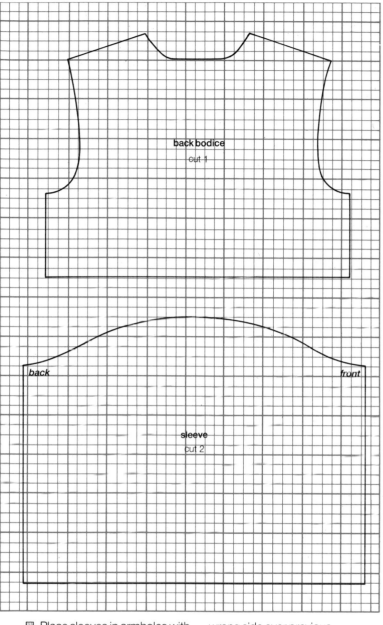

back bodice
cut 1

back

front

sleeve
cut 2

▦ Place sleeves in armholes with right sides together, matching underarm seams and pulling up gathers evenly to fit; pin and stitch in place.

▦ Work two rows of gathering stitches around base of each sleeve. Pull up gathers evenly until base measures 7in (18cm); stitch over gathers to hold in place.

▦ Fold each cuff in half; pin and stitch into a ring.

▦ Pin and stitch one edge of cuff to edge of sleeve. Turn under remaining edge and slipstitch to

wrong side over previous stitches.

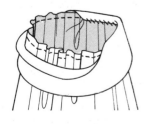

▦ Place collars with right sides together; pin and stitch leaving neck edges open. Trim and turn collar to the right side. Place one

edge of collar to neck edge with right sides together; pin and stitch. Turn under remaining raw edge and slipstitch over previous stitches.

▦ Turn skirt up to the required length, then tuck under ¼in (6mm) and hem in place.

▦ Pin and topstitch two rows of braid around base edge of skirt, ¼in (6mm) from bottom edge and ¼in (6mm) apart. Pin and topstitch two rows of braid around the collar and one row around each cuff in the same way.

▦ Work two horizontal buttonholes at center of front opening, stitching buttons to the opposite side to match. Sew a snap fastener on bodice at collar position. Tie the ribbon into a large bow and sew to dress over snap fastener.

LIKE A FEATHER IN THE WIND

These little creatures float in a pastel haze of organdy. Cut to a basic apron pattern with cross ties at the back, they have their variations, like themes in music: the yellow one has tiny pintucks on the bodice and a hem in points; deeper tucks are grouped in threes on the blue; the green one has fine tucks on frills and hem; there are scalloped edges on the red; and the pink has deep pleats and petal hems. Add a simple pair of plain pants and you have perfection plus!

Size: to fit a five- to six-year-old.

MATERIALS

DRESS	PANTS
2⅛yd (2m) of 44in (112cm) wide organdy	1yd (1m) of 36in (90cm) wide cotton poplin
One ¾in (2cm) diameter button	¾yd (60cm) of elastic
Dressmakers' pattern paper	Dressmakers' pattern paper
Matching thread	Matching thread

DIRECTIONS FOR DRESSES

▦ Draw up patterns from diagrams. Cut out following cutting instructions.

▦ Follow the diagrams for the pleat and pintucked areas on the chosen pinafore: the sections marked E are the areas to be reproduced at the base of the skirt. Fold pleats and pintucks on skirt and frills; stitch and then press downwards.

▦ If the chosen pinafore has scalloped hem and frill edges, trace off the scalloped edge from the diagram and mark on the fabric ⅜in (1cm) away from the edge. Work round the marked lines with a tight machine zigzag stitch or hand buttonhole stitch; trim away excess fabric.

▦ For the pinafore with double frills, make two pairs of frills, one 3¼in (8cm) wide and the other 2in (5cm) wide; work scalloped edges as above.

▦ If the chosen pinafore has plain hem and frill edges, turn double ⅝in (1.5cm) hems; pin and stitch.

▦ Measure up 16in (40cm) from hemmed edge of skirt and cut off excess fabric around skirt top.

▦ Turn a double ⅝in (1.5cm) hem along the side edges of the skirt;

pin and stitch.

▦ Fold the bib pleats and pintucks, following diagram for chosen pinafore and leaving ⅝in (1.5cm) at the neck edge; pin and stitch pleats and pintucks.

▦ Work two rows of gathering stitches round the base of each frill and pull up until frill measures 20in (50cm); stitch over gathers to hold. Trim until bib front measures 7in (18cm) from neck edge.

▦ With right sides together, place frills to bib; pin and tack.

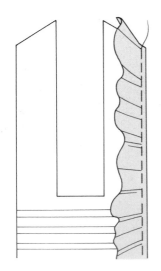

ballerinas Degas-style

▦ Place bib lining to bib with right sides together; pin and stitch neck and outer edges, catching in frills. Trim and turn to right side. Turn in raw ends of bib straps and slipstitch.

▦ Work a row of gathering stitches round the top edge of skirt and pull up to 24in (60cm); stitch over gathers to hold. With right sides together, place one waistband to skirt; pin and stitch. Fold up waistband to right side.

▦ With right sides together, place bib bottom centered to upper edge of waistband; pin and tack.

▦ With right sides together, place waistband lining to waistband; pin and stitch upper edge through all layers. Turn to right side, tuck in raw edges and slipstitch in place.

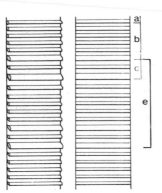

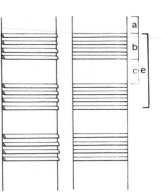

YELLOW PINAFORE a ⅛in (3mm); *b* five pintucks with ¼in (6mm) spaces; *c* one pleat ¼in (6mm), one pintuck, one ¼in (6mm) pleat.

BLUE PINAFORE a three ⅜in (1cm) pleats; *b* ¾in (2cm) spaces; *c* 1¼in (3cm)

GREEN PINAFORE a ⅝in (1.5cm); *b* four pintucks with ¼in (6mm) spaces; *c* 1in (2.5cm) space; *d* 1in (2.5cm)

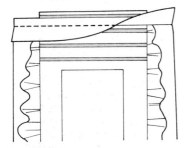

▦ Fold apron strings in half lengthwise; pin and stitch raw edges, leaving one end open. Trim and turn to right side.

▦ Make two small pleats at raw end until string measures 1½in (4cm); push ends inside waistband ends; pin and stitch to close, catching in string.

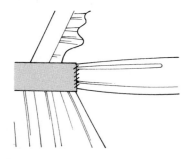

▦ Work a buttonhole at the end of each bib strap and one on the right side of the waistband. Stitch a button to the end of the left side of the waistband to match.

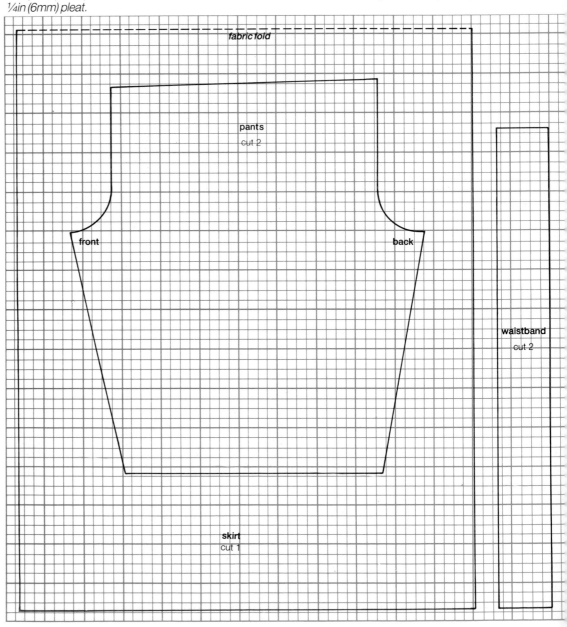

fabric fold

pants
cut 2

front

back

waistband
cut 2

skirt
cut 1

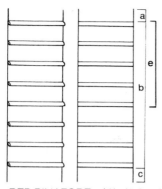

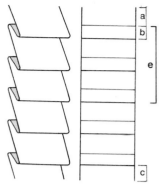

RED PINAFORE **a** ½in (1.2cm); **b** eight pintucks with ¼in (5mm) spaces; **c** ½in (1.3cm)

PINK PINAFORE **a** ¾in (2cm) space; **b** ⅜in (1cm) pleat; **c** ⅜in (1cm) space

All the pintucks are ⅛in (2mm) wide. After stitching the pintucks press them downwards.

The area marked **e** on each diagram is the pleat area to be reproduced at the base of the skirt.

DIRECTIONS FOR PANTS

▦ Draw up patterns from diagram. Cut out following cutting instructions.

▦ Place pants with right sides together; pin and stitch center and inner leg seams.

▦ Turn up a 1in (2.5cm) hem at the base of each leg, then tuck under ¼in (6mm); pin and hem in place.

▦ Turn down ¾in (2cm) at waist edge, then tuck under ¼in (6mm); pin and stitch close to edge, leaving an opening at one seam. Thread elastic through waist casing; overlap ends for ⅜in (1cm) and stitch together. Push elastic into casing and stitch up opening.

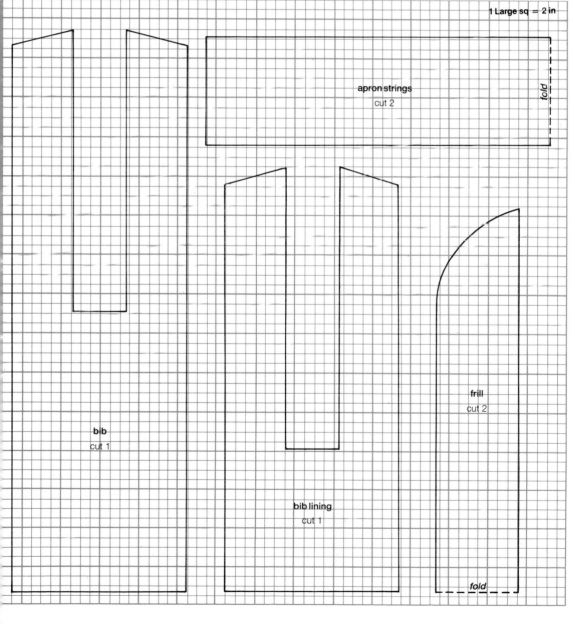

1 Large sq = 2 in

apron strings
cut 2

fold

bib
cut 1

bib lining
cut 1

frill
cut 2

fold

PARTY DRESS

Take a little extra loving care to produce a dress for a grand occasion. Classic fabrics such as crisp white eyelet embroidery invite the extra stitchery, lace appliqué and ribbon-threading that make a dress unique, nostalgic. This sleeveless masterpiece with an over-bodice flatters a girl's best features and ignores her lack of waist with tact. No one is above that kind of flattery.

Size: to fit a four-year-old.

MATERIALS

1¾yd (1.6m) of 45in (114cm) wide fine white pique
5½yd (5m) of scalloped braid (A)
2⅛yd (2m) of 1in (2.5cm) wide ribbon (B)
7¾yd (7m) of ¼in (6mm) wide lace (C)
1yd (1m) of ⅜in (1cm) wide open-work insertion (D)
½yd (40cm) of binding with picots (E)

½yd (40cm) of ¼in (6mm) wide lace (F)
10in (25cm) of ⅝in (1.5cm) wide braid (G)
4in (10cm) of flowery braid (I).
Four ½in (1.3cm) diameter buttons
Dressmakers' pattern paper
Matching thread

DIRECTIONS

▣ Draw up patterns from diagrams. Cut out following cutting instructions.
▣ Following guidelines on the pattern, place lengths of ribbon (B) on the front and back bodice, pin and stitch down the lengths. Tack lace (C) parallel to the edge of ribbons (B); pin and stitch.
▣ With right sides together, pin and stitch shoulder seams. Repeat for yoke lining. With right sides together, place the scalloped braid (A) with straight edge along the base and armhole edges of the bodice; pin and stitch. Fold scalloped edge of braid to right side of base and armhole edges, folding the raw fabric edge under to the wrong side of garment.

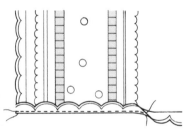

▣ Place bodice and bodice lining with right sides together; pin and stitch center back edges together. Turn to right side. Turn in seam allowance along neck edge of both bodice and bodice lining.
▣ Position braid (G) on edge of right back bodice; pin and stitch. Place binding (E) between neck edges of bodice and lining; pin and tack neck edges together. Position lace (F) round the neck edge of bodice; pin and stitch in place through all layers.

▣ Turn in lining edges and handstitch bodice and bodice lining together at armhole edges, leaving 1¾in (4.5cm) open at the

bottom to slip in the skirt.

▣ Topstitch the four lines across the front (see photograph/pattern). Cut out flowers from flowery braid (I) and stitch by hand to bodice at each intersection.

▣ Turn under narrow hems on each side of front skirt; pin and tack. Make a 1¾in (4.5cm) wide horizontal pleat round the base of the skirt, 5in (13cm) up from base edge; stitch. Position a length of ribbon (B) along each side edge of front skirt; pin and topstitch.
▣ Turn under narrow hems on sides and base of back skirt; pin and tack. Make a pleat round the back panel in the same way as for the front.
▣ Place back to back panel with right sides together, inserting open-work intersection (D); pin and stitch. Position lace (C) on either side of intersection; pin and stitch.

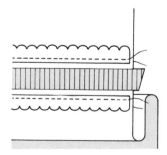

▣ To join back skirt to front, place the free edge of ribbon (B) over side of skirt; pin and topstitch. Position lace (C) along edges of ribbon (B); pin and stitch.

a special frock for a grand event

▦ To make an opening in skirt, cut a 5in (13cm) long slit in the center back of skirt, as marked on the pattern. Cut a straight strip of fabric 10¼in × 1⅜in (26cm × 3.5cm). Pin strip down one side of slit and then up the second side, keeping right sides together; stitch close to edge. Fold the strip through center to wrong side. Turn under raw edge for ⅛in (3mm) and slipstitch over previous stitching.

▦ Work a row of gathering stitches round top edge of front skirt, omitting ribbons (B); pull up gathers evenly until skirt front measures 6¼in (16cm); stitch over gathers to hold in place. Repeat at back, pulling up to 8½in (21.5cm).

▦ Place scalloped braid (A) around right side of one waistband; pin and tack. Place second waistband to first with right sides together; pin and stitch all round, catching in braid and leaving an opening for turning. Trim and turn to right side; stitch up opening.

▦ Join bodice to skirt by inserting the top 1¾in (4.5cm) of skirt between bodice and bodice lining, matching up vertical bands of front and edges of bodice to center back opening in skirt; topstitch together with a zigzag stitch.

▦ Place waistband in place 1¾in (4.5cm) up from bodice edge. Pin and stitch in place on edge of scalloped braid at the top edge and up to the bodice along the base edge.

▦ Work three vertical buttonholes on the left-hand opening on the braid and a loop at neck edge. Stitch buttons to the opposite side to match.

▦ Turn up hem to the required length, then tuck under ¼in (6mm) and hem in place.

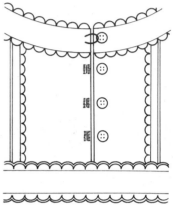

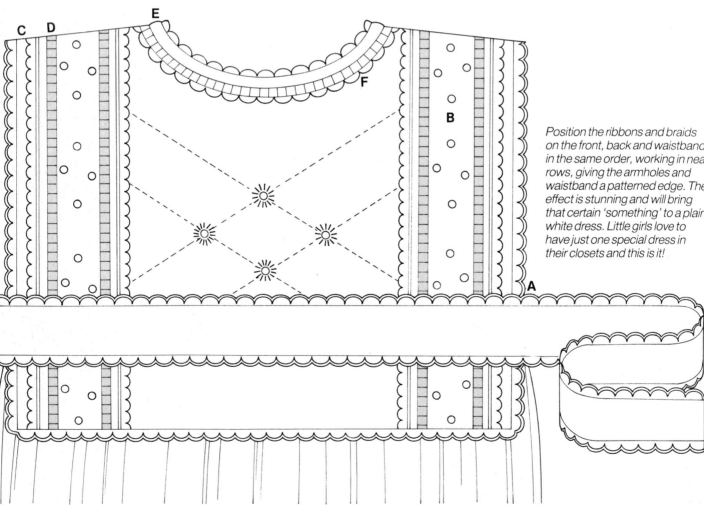

Position the ribbons and braids on the front, back and waistband in the same order, working in neat rows, giving the armholes and waistband a patterned edge. The effect is stunning and will bring that certain 'something' to a plain white dress. Little girls love to have just one special dress in their closets and this is it!

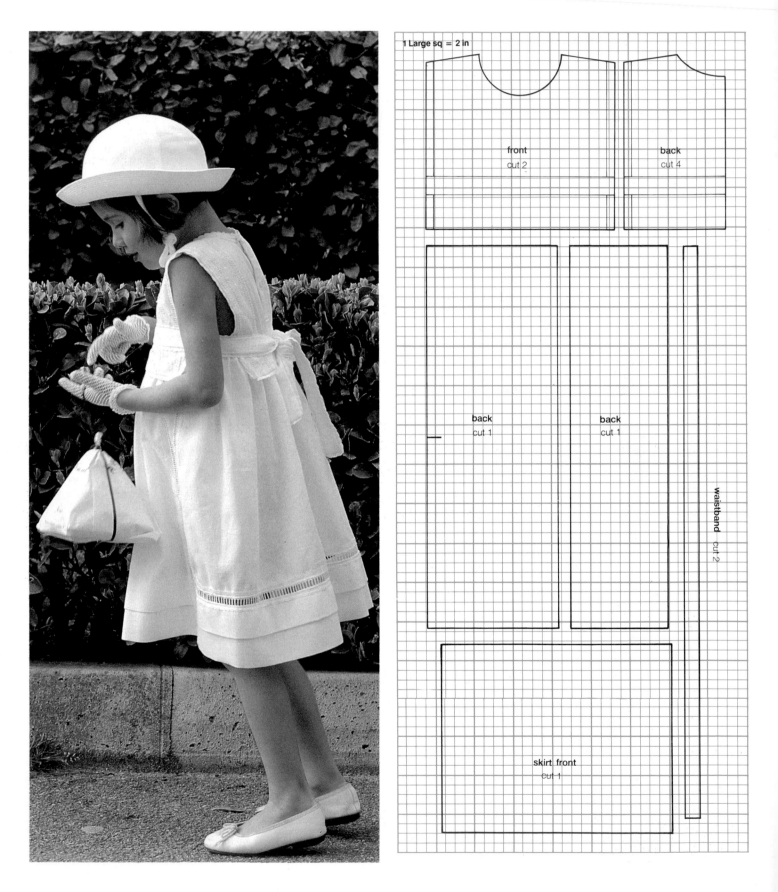

1 Large sq = 2 in

front
cut 2

back
cut 4

back
cut 1

back
cut 1

waistband cut 2

skirt front
cut 1

FULL SPEED AHEAD

A young boy's best blouson jacket for practicality and dash. Smart gray flannel keeps him warm and the generous raglan sleeves are comfortable, too. The ribbing for collar, cuffs and waistband is quick to knit and easy to stitch on. And what could be a simpler decoration than touch-and-close stripes and shapes in all colors, for the sportsman on the move? It's easy for him to open and close this jacket – after all, doesn't he like his independence at an early age?

Size: to fit a four-year-old.

MATERIALS

1yd (90cm) of 60in (150cm) wide gray flannel
Of ¾in (2cm) wide nylon tape fastening: 22in (55cm) of yellow; 25½in (65cm) of red; 30in (75cm) of blue and 10in (25cm) of green

One 2oz (50g) ball of Pingouin Pingofine in blue, red, yellow and green
One pair of size 5 (4mm) knitting needles
Dressmakers' pattern paper
Matching thread

DIRECTIONS

▦ Draw up patterns from diagrams. Cut out following cutting instructions.
▦ With right sides together, pin and stitch sleeves along upper arm seam AB. Pink the raw edges and press seams open. Topstitch ¼in (6mm) on either side of seams. Using the soft half of the nylon tape fastening, place one length of blue 3¼in (8cm) above line CD. Above it, add a length of red and then yellow, spacing each length ¾in (2cm) apart; pin and topstitch in place, using matching thread.

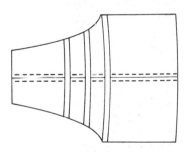

▦ With right sides together, pin and stitch sleeve to armhole edges. Pink the raw edges, press seams open and topstitch ¼in (6mm) on either side of seams.
▦ Fold jacket with right sides together; pin and stitch side seams from waist to wrist on each side. Pink the raw edges, press seams open and topstitch ¼in (6mm) on either side of seams.
▦ To finish front edges, turn in front facing on each side of jacket along marked line; pin and tack. Cut seven small squares of nylon tape fastening from all the different colors. Stitch one half of each piece to right side of right

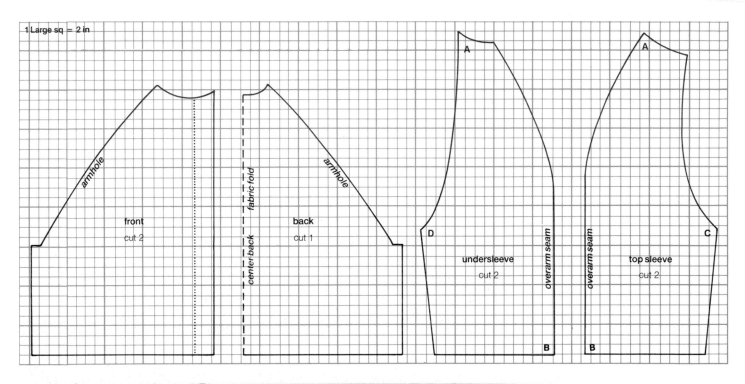

1 Large sq = 2 in

front
cut 2

armhole

fabric fold

center back

back
cut 1

armhole

A

D

undersleeve
cut 2

overarm seam

B

A

overarm seam

top sleeve
cut 2

C

B

front and the opposite halves to the underside of the left front to correspond.

▦ For lower border, cast on 136 sts in blue yarn. Work six rows of P2, K2 rib, then six rows in red, six rows in yellow and two rows in green. Bind off.

▦ For collar neckband, cast on 70 sts in blue yarn. Work two rows of P2, K2 rib, then two rows in red and two rows in yellow. Bind off.

▦ For each wristband, cast on 40sts in red yarn. Work six rows of P2, K2 rib then six rows in yellow. Bind off.

▦ Stitch the wristbands to form rings, then stitch one to lower edge of each sleeve, slightly gathering up sleeve edge evenly to fit. Stitch knitted lower band to lower edge of jacket, gathering up jacket edge evenly to fit. Stitch the knitted neckband in place around neck edge of jacket.

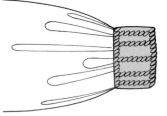

PLASTIC PRACTICALITY

Small boys love splashing through rain and puddles and they'll be well protected in this bold bright vinyl raincoat. You'll need a sharp needle for stitching the vinyl, and be sure to use tissue paper or a roller foot to help the fabric go under the presser foot. Your efforts are rewarded: there's no need to finish the edges and eyelets and no-sew snaps snap closed in seconds.

Size: to fit an eighteen-month- to two-year-old.

MATERIALS

1yd (1m) of 48in (120cm) wide patterned vinyl	¾yd (70cm) of narrow cord
	Adhesive tape
Two ¼in (6mm) diameter eyelets	Dressmakers' pattern paper
Four no-sew snap fasteners	Matching thread

DIRECTIONS

▦ Draw up patterns from diagrams. Cut out following cutting instructions.

▦ Turn down the right side of each pocket top for ¾in (2cm); hold with tape and stitch in place at sides. Snip corners and turn facing to inside the pocket.

▦ Turn under seam allowances on all remaining edges; hold with tape.

▦ Place pockets on fronts at marked positions; hold with tape and topstitch in place close to outer edges.

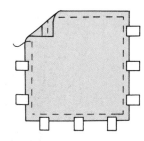

▦ Place sleeves to fronts with right sides together; hold with tape and stitch in place. Repeat, to stitch back to sleeves. Trim down seam allowances.

▦ Fold, so that back and fronts have right sides together; hold with tape and stitch side seams, continuing along underarm sleeve seams. Trim down seam allowances.

▦ Place hood pieces with right sides together; hold with tape and stitch curved seam. Trim seam allowances.

▦ Turn under front edge of hood along marked line, hold with tape and topstitch hem in place.

▦ Fix an eyelet into hood on each side at marked positions, following manufacturer's instructions. Place hood to neck edge, with right sides together and front edges of hood to center front; hold with tape and stitch in place. Trim seam allowances.

▦ Turn under a 1in (2.5cm) hem at the base of each sleeve; hold with tape; and topstitch in place. Stitch a similar hem along base edge of coat.

▦ Turn in facing along marked lines; topstitch in place. Turn under neck and hem edge and handstitch.

▦ Fix no-sew snap fasteners in place at marked positions, following manufacturer's instructions.

▦ Thread cord through eyelets in hood and knot both ends.

for rainy day appointments

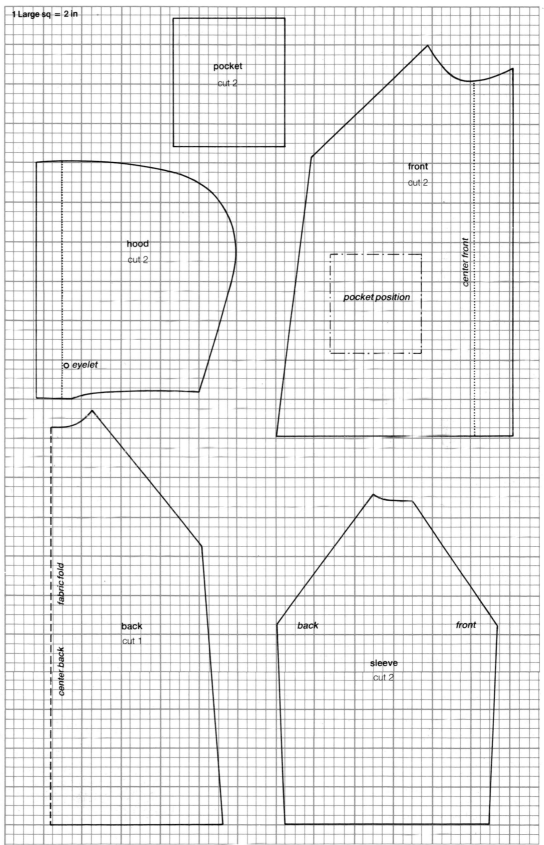

1 Large sq = 2 in

pocket
cut 2

front
cut 2

center front

hood
cut 2

pocket position

o eyelet

fabric fold

back
cut 1

center back

back

front

sleeve
cut 2

PATCHWORK PARKAS

With large lined hoods and pockets big enough for everyone's special objects, these parkas are the perfect solution to the cold outdoors. Make them in red, blue, green and yellow – with such sizzling colors, who says winter exercise needs to be a chore? Choose your own color combinations to suit each member of the family. In strong canvas with a drawstring at the waist, they are cut big enough to last youngsters a good few years.

Size: to fit a four-year-old or twelve-year-old.

MATERIALS

60in (150cm) wide canvas – work out how much you need in each color by drawing up the patterns and then making a cutting plan	*Four ⅜in (8mm) diameter eyelets*
	1⅝yd (1.5m) of 1in (2.5cm) wide bias binding (four-year-old) or
	1⅞yd (1.7m) of 1in (2.5cm) wide bias binding (twelve-year-old)
2⅛yd (2m) of cord (four-year-old) or 2¾yd (2.5m) of cord (twelve-year-old)	*½in (1.3cm) wide bias binding, for binding pockets*
Eight no-sew snap fasteners	*Dressmakers' pattern paper*
	Matching thread

DIRECTIONS

▦ Draw up patterns from diagram. Cut out from the desired colors.

▦ Join all the sections together with flat fell seams, unless otherwise stated.

▦ Place upper backs with right sides together; pin and stitch center back seam.

▦ Pin upper back to lower back and stitch. Pin upper fronts to lower fronts and stitch.

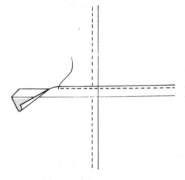

▦ Mark each pocket position with rows of tacking stitches: one row around the pocket position and one across the center.

▦ Fold welt in half lengthwise with right sides together; pin and stitch sides with plain seams. Trim and turn to right side.

▦ Pin and tack welt to front, along marked lower pocket line, with right sides together and raw edges to center line. Place one pocket lining right side down over welt, pin and stitch through all layers along lower marked line.

▦ Place second pocket lining right side down in position along top marked line, overlapping lower stitching line by ¼in (6mm); pin and stitch in place along top marked line.

▦ Cut along pocket center line to within ¼in (6mm) of ends, then cut into each corner. Turn pocket linings through opening to wrong side and press; pin and stitch linings together, leaving edges at center front of jacket free (these will be stitched together with the jacket).

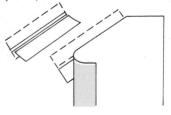

Large Parka

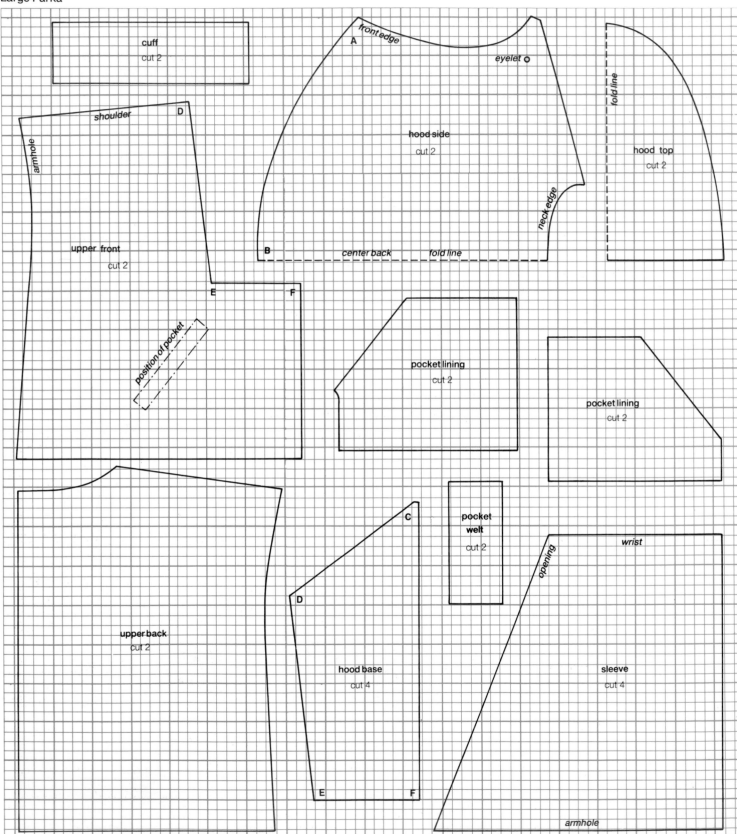

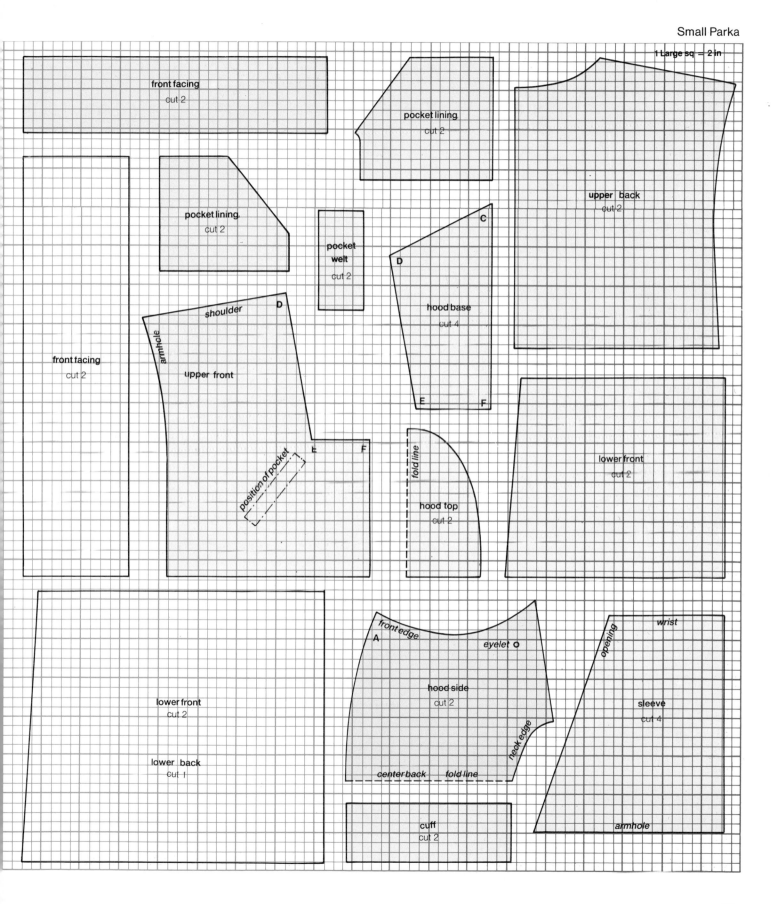

▦ Fold bias binding evenly in half over raw edges of pocket lining, omitting center front edges; pin and stitch.

▦ On right side, fold up welt; pin and top stitch to jacket at both ends. Repeat to make up second pocket in the same way.

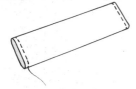

▦ Place fronts to back; pin and stitch shoulder seams. Place sleeves to front/back with right sides together; pin and stitch. Fold front to back with right sides together; pin and stitch side seams, continuing stitching along underarm seam of sleeve, ending 3¼in (8cm) from wrist to allow for wrist opening.

▦ Turn under a narrow double hem along either side of each sleeve opening; pin and stitch. Fold a series of knife pleats along base of sleeve, so that sleeve base fits cuff; pin and tack in place.

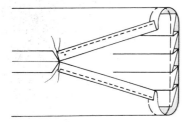

▦ Fold each cuff in half lengthwise with right sides together; pin and stitch sides with plain seams. Trim and turn cuff to right side.

▦ Pin one raw edge of cuff to base of each sleeve with right sides together and stitch with plain seam. Turn in remaining raw edge of cuff and pin and topstitch in place.

▦ Place hood side to hood top with right sides together; pin and stitch with plain seams from A to B. Place hood to hood bases with right sides together; pin and stitch with plain seams from C to D. Repeat with hood lining

pieces, and then stitch front facings to edges of hood base lining.

▦ Fix two eyelets in hood edge at marked positions, following manufacturer's instructions.

▦ Join hood to jacket at each side, F to E to D to D to E to F with plain seams. Pin hood lining/facing to jacket hood with right sides together; using plain seams, stitch around front edges of jacket and hood, catching in raw front edges of pocket. Trim and turn to inside. Finish raw edges of facings and handstitch in place around hood. Topstitch around hood to resemble a flat fell seam.

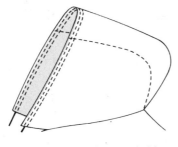

▦ Make a casing by topstitching two rows, ¾in (2cm) and ⅝in (1.5cm) from edges of front hood. Thread cord round casing from eyelet to eyelet. Knot ends.

▦ Fix two eyelets in position through jacket only (not facing) at waistline, 1½in (4cm) from front edges.

▦ Open out bias binding and place flat around jacket at waistline to provide a casing; pin and topstitch in place. Thread cord round casing from eyelet to eyelet. Knot ends.

▦ Turn up lower edges of parka, including facing edges, to form a double ¾in (2cm) hem; pin and topstitch in place.

▦ Fix no-sew snap fasteners down center front edges and on each cuff, following manufacturer's instructions.

THE SQUARE BAND

Bold squares look great on these ample jackets that are just the job for the whole gang when the weather turns cold. Lumberjack styling with leather buttons and leather-trimmed pockets give these jackets a rugged grown-up look. The lining in brushed cotton makes them all the warmer.

Size: to fit a three-year-old.

MATERIALS

1yd (1m) of 45in (114cm) wide checked wool fabric
¾yd (70cm) of 36in (90cm) wide brushed cotton or fine wool for lining
4in (10cm) of 54in (140cm) wide imitation leather
6in (15cm) of 54in (140cm) wide fur fabric

Five ¾in (2cm) diameter imitation leather buttons
Two ⅜in (1cm) diameter imitation leather buttons
Dressmakers' pattern paper
Matching thread

DIRECTIONS

▦ Draw up patterns from diagrams. Cut out following cutting instructions.

▦ For pocket piping, cut eight strips of imitation leather, each 5⅛in × 1¼in (13cm × 3cm). For bottom pocket flaps, cut out four pieces of woolen fabric each 5⅛in × 2½in (13cm × 6.5cm). For pocket linings, cut out four pieces of lining fabric each 5⅛in × 9in (13cm × 23cm). Tack a line ½in (1.3cm) below center across lining to mark position of slit. Mark stitching lines on jacket and lining. Mark slit line on jacket.

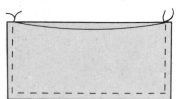

▦ Place two pocket flaps with right sides together; pin and stitch both sides and one long edge. Trim and turn to right side.

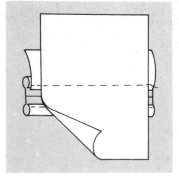

▦ Fold two piping strips in half

lengthwise with wrong sides together; pin and tack strips along both sides of slit on stitching lines at each base pocket position, with raw edges facing.

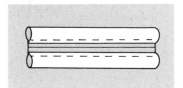

▦ Place flap over top stitching line, with raw edge facing slit, and tack; then place pocket lining over flap, matching stitching lines and with longer side of lining above the slit line. Stitch through all layers along stitching lines and across both ends. Cut along slit line to within ¼in (6mm) of each end; snip into corners.

cosy comfort for small lumberjacks

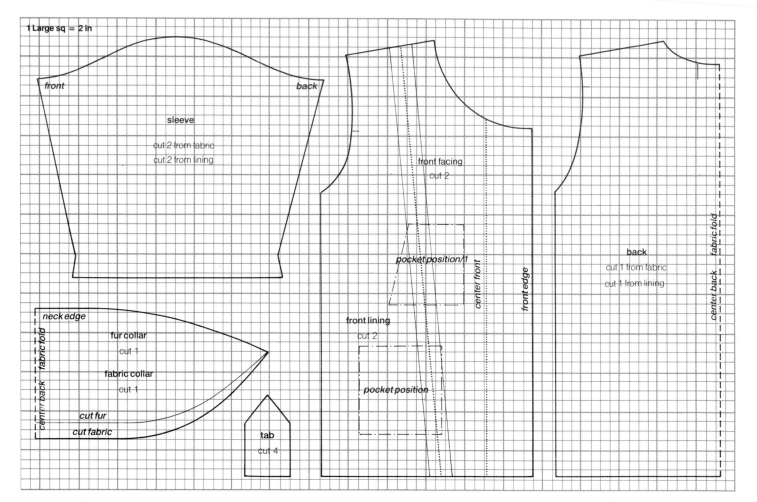

1 Large sq = 2 in

front

back

sleeve

cut 2 from fabric
cut 2 from lining

front facing
cut 2

pocket position/1

center front

front edge

back

cut 1 from fabric
cut 1 from lining

center back

fabric fold

neck edge

fabric fold

center back

fur collar
cut 1

fabric collar
cut 1

cut fur

cut fabric

front lining
cut 2

pocket position

tab
cut 4

▥ Push piping and lining through slit. Form an even piping on right side and topstitch along seam line.

▥ Fold top part of pocket lining over lower part, keeping it free from jacket and flap; pin and stitch to form pocket. Trim and finish.

▥ Make top pockets in the same way, omitting flaps and slanting pocket sides (see photograph).

▥ From imitation leather, cut eight triangles, each with two sides 1¼in (3cm) long, and a 1½in (4cm) long base. Topstitch one at each end of pocket slits.

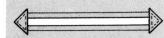

▥ From imitation leather, cut two strips each 10½in × ⅝in (27cm × 1.5cm). Position a strip across each front at armhole level; pin and topstitch in place.

▥ Place fronts to back with right sides together; pin and stitch shoulder seams. Place sleeves with right side to front/back; pin and stitch in place.

▥ To make up each sleeve tab: place two tab pieces with right sides together; pin and stitch together, leaving short straight edges open. Trim and turn to right side. Topstitch close to outer edge.

▥ Pin each tab on sleeve, with raw edges along side seam, 2½in (6cm) up from wrist.

▥ Fold jacket so that front and back have right sides together; pin and stitch side seams, continuing stitching along underarm seams of sleeves, catching in tabs. Trim and edge-finish.

▥ Pin and stitch front facings to linings, then make up lining in the same way as jacket, omitting tabs and pockets.

▥ With right sides together, pin and stitch fur collar to neck edge of lining. With right sides together, pin and stitch fabric collar to neck edge of fabric jacket.

▥ To make up three button loops, cut three strips of imitation leather, each 3¼in × ⅝in (8cm × 1.5cm). Fold strips in half lengthwise with wrong sides together; topstitch down length close to edge. Fold into loops and pin to left front, 1½in (4cm), 5⅛in (13cm) and 8¾in (22cm) from neck edges; tack.

▥ With right sides together, place lining to jacket. Pin and stitch together from base of right front around to base of left front,

catching in button loops and continuing around collar. Trim and turn to right side. Topstitch front ¼in (6mm) from edges.

▥ At outer edge of collar, press in fur collar for about ¼in (6mm). Topstitch along seam to hold in place.

▥ Push lining sleeves down into fabric sleeves, then turn up both hems to inside along marked line; pin and topstitch together. Finish base edge of jacket in the same way.

▥ Stitch three large buttons to jacket right front to match loops, and two large buttons on the left side in line with loops.

▥ Fold sleeve tabs on sleeves and stitch ends in place through smaller buttons.

PARTY PURSES

Little girls seem to need an endless supply of purses, bags and cases to keep their favorite trinkets. One of these would make the perfect present for a birthday or for Christmas. All you need are two squares of fabric, scraps for the features, and embroidery silks to make your own versions of these great ideas.

MATERIALS FOR CAT BAG

Piece of black fur fabric 16in ×
  12in (40cm × 30cm)
Scraps of gray fur fabric
Scraps of pink leather
One pair of glass eyes
26in (65cm) of black cord

White nylon thread
8in (20cm) of 36in (90cm) wide
  lining fabric
Fabric glue
Matching thread

DIRECTIONS FOR CAT BAG

▦ Draw up patterns from diagram. Cut out following cutting instructions.

▦ Fix the glass eyes in bag front at marked positions. Cut whiskers from nylon thread and position ends at marked nose position. Glue nose in place over whiskers; slipstitch in place.

▦ Place ears together in pairs: one gray ear to one black ear with right sides together; pin and stitch all round, leaving base edges open. Trim and turn to right side. Place on bag front at marked positions. Pin each end of cord strap at marked positions.

▦ Place bag back to bag front with right sides together; pin and stitch together, catching in ears and cord ends and leaving an opening at top edge. Trim and turn to right side.

▦ Make up lining and stitch to bag in the same way as for sheep bag.

MATERIALS FOR RUSSIAN DOLL

⅝yd (50cm) of 36in (90cm) wide
  cotton fabric
⅝yd (50cm) of 36in (90cm) wide
  printed cotton fabric
Pieces of wadding

Embroidery cottons and machine
  embroidery threads
Scrap of pink felt
Assortment of braids
Matching thread

DIRECTIONS FOR RUSSIAN DOLL

▦ Draw up patterns from diagrams. Cut out following cutting instructions.

▦ Place upper bag pieces in position on main doll bag as shown in diagram; pin and stitch.

▦ Position gussets to each side of main bag piece with right sides together; pin and stitch.

▦ Embroider the face with straight stitches and French knots, adding small pink felt circles for cheeks. Embroider hands at each side and a braid of hair at the back.

▦ Position a length of decorative braid on each side of bag where upper bag piece ends; pin and stitch in place, adding rows of machine embroidery stitches above the braid.

▦ For the lining, join gussets to main bag piece as above, leaving an opening in one seam. Place lining to bag with right sides together; pin and stitch around bag top. Trim and turn to right side. Turn in opening; slipstitch to close.

▦ Cut a 25½in (65cm) length of braid for the handle; tuck under raw ends and stitch to each side.

▦ Make up two more dolls with embroidered fronts and printed cotton backs, with a layer of wadding inside.

▦ On the front of the smaller doll, position a length of embroidered ribbon to form a pocket; stitch base and sides.

▦ Place dolls one on top of the other; stitch base and sides, leaving openings at the top, so that they form pockets.

MATERIALS FOR PIGGY

Piece of pink leather 12in × 28in (30cm × 70cm)	*5in (13cm) zipper* *Suitable filling* *Matching thread*

DIRECTIONS FOR PIGGY

▦ Draw up patterns from diagrams. Cut out following cutting instructions.

▦ Cut out a 3in (7.5cm) wide gusset to fit all round bag front and back. Stitch gusset ends together to form a ring. Cut a 4⅜in (11cm) long slit at center of gusset. Position zipper in slit; stitch in place.

▦ On bag front, make two small holes for eyes. Cut out nostril shapes from muzzle. Position muzzle to bag front; topstitch in place.

▦ Place gusset to bag front with zipper placed at center top; topstitch in place. Make a ¾in (2cm) slit across gusset on sides of zipper.

▦ Cut a strap 26in × ¾in (65cm × 2cm) from leather. Insert ends through slits at sides of zipper and topstitch in place. Open zipper. Topstitch bag back to opposite side of gusset.

▦ Place ears in pairs with wrong sides together; topstitch, adding a small amount of filling inside each one. Place ears to sides of bag and topstitch in place.

Imitate the wooden Russian dolls with embroidered clothes and features. The graduating size of the dolls is effectively reproduced by the two doll pockets.

A pink leather pig is just the answer for carrying around all the valuables. The zipper opening is set into the gusset top and wide shoulder strap ends slot in at each side before being stitched in place, to give practicality to a fun idea.

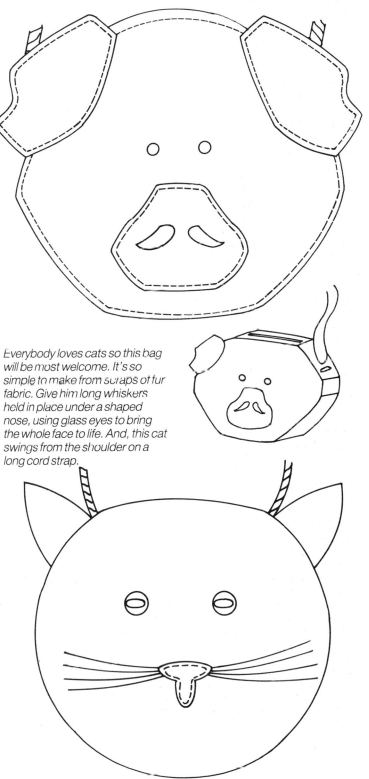

Everybody loves cats so this bag will be most welcome. It's so simple to make from scraps of fur fabric. Give him long whiskers held in place under a shaped nose, using glass eyes to bring the whole face to life. And, this cat swings from the shoulder on a long cord strap.

71

MATERIALS FOR JAM POT

⅝yd (50cm) of 36in (90cm) wide
   gingham
1⅝yd (1.5m) of ¾in (2cm) wide
   heavy ribbon
Small piece of wadding

25½in (65cm) of 1in (2.5cm) wide
   bias binding
Embroidery cotton
Matching thread

DIRECTIONS FOR JAM POT

▦ Draw up patterns from diagram. Cut out following cutting instructions.

▦ Position lengths of heavy ribbon side by side to cover bag pieces; pin and topstitch in place. Place bag pieces with right sides together; pin and stitch side seams.

▦ Cut out a circle of gingham to fit base. Place base to sides with wrong sides together; pin and stitch around base. Trim.

▦ Fold bias binding over raw edges of base; pin and topstitch in place.

▦ Overlap side edges of wadded pieces; pin and stitch together. Cut out and stitch a wadding base to wadded sides. Place inside bag.

▦ Pin and stitch lining together in the same way.

▦ Cut a 2in (5cm) wide strip of gingham 1½ times the circumference of the bag; pin and stitch short ends together, to form a ring. Turn under a double ¼in (6mm) hem; pin and stitch. Work a row of gathering stitches along opposite edge. Pull up gathers evenly and pin to top edge of ribboned bag, with wrong sides together ½in (1.3cm) down from edge; stitch in place.

▦ Place lining inside bag, with wrong sides together; turn lining over at top edge to form a ¾in (2cm) wide band, then turn under raw edge; pin and slipstitch.

▦ Embroider around the label using buttonhole stitch. Pin label to bag front; stitch in place with buttonhole stitch.

▦ For handle, cut a 25½in (65cm) strip of binding. Fold in half lengthwise; pin and topstitch all round. Place to each side of bag; stitch in place.

A pot of jam can hide a variety of secrets. Lengths of braid make up the pot and shoulder strap, the top has a cheerful gingham cover.

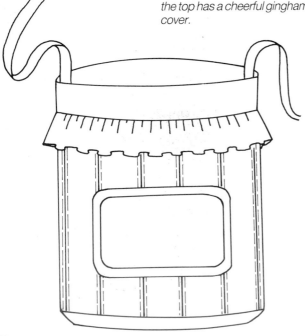

MATERIALS FOR SHEEP BAG

Piece of white fur fabric 16in ×
  8in (40cm × 20cm)
Piece of pink leather
25½in (65cm) pink cord
8in (20cm) of 36in (90cm) wide
  lining fabric

One pair of glass eyes
Suitable filling
Embroidery cotton
Matching thread

MATERIALS FOR ARTISTS' PALETTE

⅝yd (50cm) of 36in (90cm) wide
  canvas
Odds and ends of cotton poplin
  fabric in different colors
Iron-on fabric

⅝yd (1.5cm) of ½in (1.3cm) wide
  bias binding
Embroidery cottons
Matching thread

DIRECTIONS FOR SHEEP

▥ Draw up patterns from diagram. Cut out following cutting instructions.

▥ Place nose to muzzle; pin and topstitch in place. Embroider mouth in gray. Place muzzle to front of bag; pin and slipstitch in place, adding a small amount of filling.

▥ Fix glass eyes in place above muzzle. Place two ears with right sides together; pin and stitch, leaving base edges open. Trim and turn to right side. Add a little filling and pin in position on bag front.

▥ Place bag back to bag front with right sides together; pin and stitch, catching in ears, and leaving top edge open. Trim and turn to right side.

▥ For lining, place back to front with right sides together; pin and stitch, leaving top edge free and an opening in one side.

▥ Pin ends of cord to either side of head (see photograph).

▥ Place lining to bag with right sides together; pin and stitch together around top, catching in cord ends. Trim and turn to right side. Turn in opening edges; pin and slipstitch together to close. Push lining down inside bag.

DIRECTIONS FOR PALETTE

▥ Draw up patterns from diagram. Cut out following cutting instructions.

▥ Place back pieces with wrong sides together; pin and tack. Repeat with front pieces.

▥ On bag front, cut out marked hole and buttonhole stitch all round the outer edge to finish.

▥ Press iron-on fabric to odds and ends of colored fabric.

▥ Cut out each paint shape. Position on bag front and press in place. Stitch all round. Embroider paintbrushes.

▥ Fold bias binding over the outer edges of both bag front and bag back; pin and topstitch in place.

▥ Place back and front bag pieces with wrong sides together; pin and stitch together, following previous stitching lines and leaving top edge open.

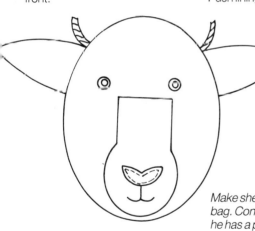

Make sheep's eyes with this fun bag. Constructed from fur fabric he has a pink leather nose.

This clutch bag has a thumb hold. Odds and ends of plain cottons provide the colorful 'paints' alongside embroidered paint brushes.

VERSATILE COLLARS

Smart little collars for a precious baby. They are quickly made – just cut out two layers of fine-quality cotton following the patterns shown and finish the inside neck edge with bias binding.

MATERIALS

PLAIN COLLARS
8in (20cm) of 36in (90cm) wide
    fabric
Scraps of iron-on interfacing
One ⅝in (1.5cm) diameter button
Matching thread

PLEATED COLLAR
8in (20cm) of 36in (90cm) wide
    printed cotton fabric
One ⅝in (1.5cm) diameter button
Matching thread

EYELET EMBROIDERY TOP
⅓yd (30cm) of 36in (90cm) wide
    eyelet embroidery
2⅛yd (2m) of ½in (1.3cm) wide bias
    binding
One ⅝in (1.5cm) diameter button
Matching thread

DIRECTIONS

Plain collar

▨ Draw up the pattern from the diagram following the lines for the desired edge. Cut out twice from fabric, adding a ⅝in (1.5cm) seam allowance all round; cut out once from iron-on interfacing. Position interfacing adhesive-side down centered on wrong side of one collar piece; press in place.

▨ Place collar pieces with right sides together; pin and stitch round edge of interfacing, leaving an opening at one back edge. Trim and turn to the right side. Turn in seam allowance along open back edge; slipstitch to close.

▨ Work a button loop on the right-hand side of the back collar. Stitch a button to the left-hand side of the collar to correspond.

Pleated collar

▨ Cut a strip of fabric 34½in × 3in (86cm × 7.5cm). Turn under a ⅝in (1.5cm) hem, then tuck under raw edge for ¼in (6mm); pin and hem in place.

▨ Fold collar into ¼in (6mm) knife pleats; pin and tack.

▨ Cut a 1in (2.5cm) wide strip of self-fabric on the bias the length of the neck edge. Place one edge of bias strip to right side of pleated collar; pin and stitch. Fold strip to wrong side over raw edge of collar, then tuck under raw

ends; pin and slipstitch in place over previous stitches.

▨ Fasten the collar at the back edge with button loop and button, as for previous collar.

Eyelet embroidery top

▨ Draw up the pattern from the diagram. Cut out once from fabric adding ½in (1.3cm) all round outer edge and ⅝in (1.5cm) round neck edge.

▨ Turn under a double ¼in (6mm) wide hem all round the outer edge. Pin and stitch in place, folding neat corners.

▨ Unfold bias binding and place one edge with right side to neck edge of collar; pin and stitch. Turn binding to wrong side, then tuck under raw ends; pin and slipstitch remaining edge in place.

▨ Fasten the collar at the back edge with button loop and button, as for previous collars.

▨ To make up ties, cut four 12in (30cm) pieces of binding. Fold each piece in half lengthwise, then tuck in raw ends; pin and topstitch all round. Stitch to each corner.

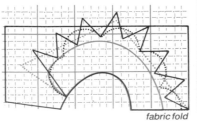

fabric fold

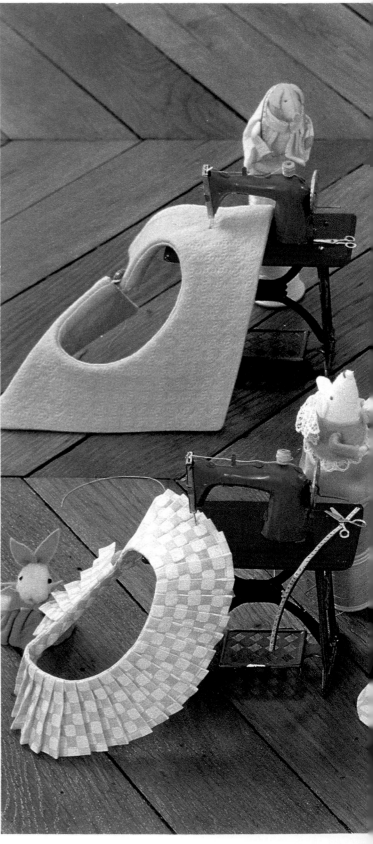

74

APPLIQUÉ TRICKS

What child doesn't love animals with a passion. One – if not all – of these creatures will be sure to be an instant success. Transform classic clothes with personal favorites: rabbits, mice, puppies and cats can all be cut out of scraps of fabric and appliquéd wherever you choose – follow the patterns and surprise them peeking out of pockets.

MATERIALS

CAT AND MOUSE
Tracing paper
Scraps of gray, white, green and printed fabric
One skein of DMC embroidery silk in each of the following colors: **white, black** *310,* **gray** *415,* **gray** *414,* **red** *666,* **green** *907,* **blue** *996,* **pink** *3689,* **pink** *760 and* **dark brown** *433*
Matching thread

RABBITS
Tracing paper
Scraps of dark brown, black, gray and beige fabric
One skein of DMC embroidery silk in each of the following colors: **white, gray** *413,* **gray** *415,* **pink** *754,* **green** *704,* **blue** *518,* **orange** *741 and* **orange** *970*
Matching thread

DOGS
Tracing paper
Scraps of dark brown, black, gray and beige fabric
One skein of DMC embroidery silk in each of the following colors: **white, black** *310,* **green** *907,* **green** *987,* **green** *967,* **blue** *518,* **pink** *3689 and* **gray** *414*
Matching thread

DIRECTIONS

▣ Trace off each section of the desired motif and cut out. Pin the motif patterns to the right side of the chosen fabrics (see photograph) and mark around the outer edge, and then mark an allowance of 1/8in (3mm) all round each shape. Cut out outside the marked areas.

▣ Staystitch, with small stitches, all round the motif pieces, just outside the inner marked line. Cut out each piece along outer marked line, cutting into curves and corners and across points.

▣ Turn under allowance all round each piece and tack.

▣ Place motif pieces on background, fitting them together by slightly overlapping the edges; pin and tack. Slipstitch each piece in place by hand.

▣ Embroider the remaining parts of the animals, using straight stitch and stem stitch. Halve the embroidery skein when stitching muzzle, eyes, whiskers and claws.

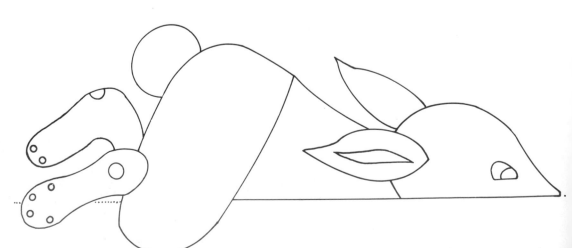

all creatures great and small

Hopping, skipping or just jumping, these little animals will bring the plainest of garments to life – give them textured fabric bodies and embroider their mischievous features.

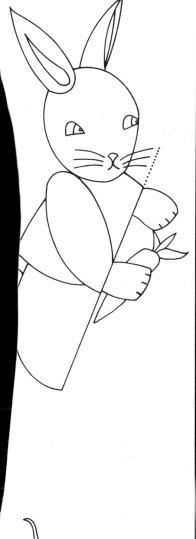

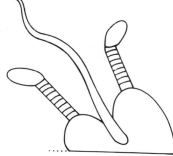

Page	Acknowledgments (Photographer/Stylist)
8,11	Marcel Duffas/Caroline Lebeau
15,17	Gilles de Chabaneix/Catherine de Chabaneix
19,21	Jerome Tisné/Isabelle Garçon
23,24,25	Gilles de Chabaneix/Marion Faver
27,28,31,32	Gilles de Chabaneix/Catherine de Chabaneix
34	Gilles de Chabaneix/Catherine de Chabaneix
36	Jerome Tisné/Caroline Lebeau
39,40	Gilles de Chabaneix/Catherine de Chabaneix
42	Daniel Burgi/Anne Luntz
43,45	Jerome Tisné/Isabelle Garçon
47,49	Jacques Dirand/Anne Luntz
50,51,53,54	Daniel Burgi/Isabelle Garçon
55,56,57	Gilles de Chabaneix/Catherine de Chabaneix
58	Gilles de Chabaneix/Catherine de Chabaneix
61,64,65	Bernard Maltaverne/Caroline Lebeau
67	Gilles de Chabaneix/Catherine de Chabaneix
69,70,72,73	Alex Bianchi/Jannick Schoumacher
75	Gilles de Chabaneix/Catherine de Chabaneix
76,77,78,79	Jerome Tisné/Isabelle Garçon